UNCOVERING

the Love

OF

Jesus

A
LENT
Devotional

UNCOVERING

the Love

OF

Jesus

ASHERITAH CIUCIU

MOODY PUBLISHERS
CHICAGO

Published in association with Literary Agent Tawny Johnson of D. C. Jacobson & Associates LLC, 537 SE Ash Street, Suite 203, Portland, OR 97214.

Details of some stories have been changed to protect the privacy of individuals. Names and/or details have been modified in the book.

Edited by Amanda Cleary Eastep
Interior Design: Puckett Smartt
Cover Design: Faceout Studio and Connie Gabbert
Cover photo of flowers copyright © 2016 by Sara K Byrne / Stocksy (965116). All rights reserved.
Cover illustration of stars copyright © 2018 by AF studio / Shutterstock (376671271). All rights reserved.
Author photo: Ashley McComb Productions

All websites and phone numbers listed herein are accurate at the time of publication but may change in the future or cease to exist. The listing of website references and resources does not imply publisher endorsement of the site's entire contents. Groups and organizations are listed for informational purposes, and listing does not imply publisher endorsement of their activities.

ISBN: 978-0-8024-1949-1

Originally delivered by fleets of horse-drawn wagons, the affordable paperbacks from D. L. Moody's publishing house resourced the church and served everyday people. Now, after more than 125 years of publishing and ministry, Moody Publishers' mission remains the same—even if our delivery systems have changed a bit.

For more information on other books (and resources) created from a biblical perspective, go to: www.moodypublishers.com or write to:

Moody Publishers
820 N. LaSalle Boulevard
Chicago, IL 60610

1 3 5 7 9 10 8 6 4 2

Printed in the United States of America

CONTENTS

WHY OBSERVE LENT?

What are you giving up for Lent?"

The first time I heard that question my freshman year of college, I shrugged it off.

Lent? Huh? Isn't that something other denominations observed to practice penitence? Why would students at this evangelical college care about that? And anyway, I had grown up in a church where we didn't do that sort of thing. We believed that salvation is a free gift of God. No self-sacrifice required.

But I was surrounded by friends who were all giving something up for Lent—sugar, Facebook, *The Bachelor*—and this ancient tradition became a rite of passage for young adults who were breaking the shackles of their conservative upbringing, eager to "make their faith their own."

So I caved in to the peer pressure, and I gave up sugar.

I'm not quite sure what I expected—perhaps a renewed spiritual vigor or a deeper understanding of God—but by Easter, I had experienced none of that. I had simply lost five pounds that quickly reappeared after a few days reacquainting myself with donuts and Mountain Dew.

It was quite the letdown.

CAN LENT REALLY BRING YOU CLOSER TO GOD?

Despite the resurgence of interest in rituals and traditions among evangelical millennials, Lent is not new, nor does it belong to any particular denomination. Historical records reveal the church has been observing a period of fasting and preparation before Resurrection Sunday since the time of the apostles, though it wasn't formalized as a universal practice until the First Council of Nicaea in AD 325.[1]

Over time, some turned Lent into an obligation rather than an invitation, and others responded by violently rejecting rituals that hinted at works-based salvation, leaving us hundreds of years later scrambling for some semblance of rhythm that will ground us in our Christian walk.

Too many of us feel like Easter kind of sneaks up on us, and we're left spiritually and emotionally unprepared to celebrate this most glorious of all celebrations: Jesus' death and resurrection as victorious King.

Is it possible, then, that we might reclaim this season of Lent to focus our hearts on Jesus in preparation for Easter Sunday? Can we leave behind the trappings of ritual that weigh down our souls and reimagine what Lent could look like for twenty-first-century Christians who sincerely love Jesus and want to seek Him with all their hearts?

I believe we can.

Lent itself will not bring you closer to God. But in the hands of our heavenly Father, Lent becomes an invitation to uncover the love of Jesus, in a far greater way than we had ever imagined.

HOW TO OBSERVE LENT WITH THIS BOOK

My hope is that as you read this book, you will uncover the deep love of Jesus poured out toward you personally in a whole new way, and that you will be a conduit of His love poured out toward those around you.

You will find some creative ideas to observe Lent throughout this devotional, including:

Daily Devotions—The daily devotions throughout this book invite us to reflect on Jesus' personal interactions with people from all walks of life. We will look at some of the ways in which Jesus lived out love as described in 1 Corinthians 13. We'll reflect on how Jesus loved others when He walked this earth, and how He demonstrates His love toward us today. Each day begins with a theme verse or two, followed by "Read the Story," an indication of where you can open your Bible to read that day's narrative from one of the Gospels. At the end of the devotional, you'll find a challenge to help you apply what you've learned of Jesus' love that day, as well as a prayer to respond to Him, and verses for further study.

Family Celebrations—The beginning of each week's devotions begins with a family celebration because Sundays are meant to be celebratory even in the midst of this otherwise somber season of Lent. These celebrations include a prayer each week, a suggested song to sing together, and other ways to worship. As Lenten Sundays traditionally do not have weekly themes associated with them, I've framed the weekly celebrations in the form of questions and answers surrounding the purpose of Jesus' death. There are many reasons Jesus came to die; I'm hoping the eight reasons I've listed throughout this book will provide a springboard into your own personal study and deeper conversations on this topic.[2]

The family celebrations also include the lighting and progressive snuffing of Lenten wreath candles, which is optional but may prove helpful for those with little children, as it provides a visual countdown toward Easter Sunday. You can find multiple options for purchasing a Lenten wreath as well as tutorials for making one at home at uncoveringthelove.com.

Activities—There are many beautiful traditions associated with Lent, and a few disciplines that are frequently practiced during this season. I've included suggestions for individual and family activities that will help you reframe this season in light of who Jesus is and what He has done; you'll find these activities at the end of each week's devotions. I've included ideas for fasting, prayer, and giving—the three disciplines traditionally associated with this season—as well as hands-on crafts for families with little ones and service activities for all ages. Incorporate the activities that best fit your interests and season of life; the only requirement here is a sincere and humble heart.

Lent is a season of somberness, a time in which we come face-to-face with our frailty as humans, our sinfulness apart from Christ, and our mortality in this body of death.[3] We grieve the brokenness in this world, and we cry out against the injustices we see around us. We mourn and lament sickness and death and cry out for forgiveness and deliverance from the sins that plague our own souls.

Quite frankly, Lent is not a fun season. It's heavy. But it's beautiful too, precisely in its permission to recognize that the Christian life is not all smiles and sunshine. In this world, we will have trouble, Jesus promises, and the season of Lent permits us to be honest about those troubles, even as we press on toward Easter Sunday with the hope that Jesus has overcome the world.

I pray you will see and savor Jesus in a fresh way in the Gospels and in your life, and that your love for Him would "abound" more and more in knowledge and depth of insight (Phil. 1:9), that He would become more precious to you, and that you would find yourself utterly enraptured with Him in a way that compels you to give of yourself toward others.

WHAT SHOULD I
SACRIFICE FOR LENT?

L et's be honest: it's infinitely easier to give up fancy coffee than it is to love that family member who wounded you in childhood. It's easier to cut a check to your favorite charity than it is to sacrifice your time and energy.

Yet sacrificial love is precisely the heart of Lent because Easter is the story of Jesus' love poured out for us.

Over the next few weeks, I invite you to join me in uncovering the love of Jesus—poured out for us, yes, but also flowing out toward others. As we follow Jesus' footsteps in sacrificing our own comforts, our own desire to be seen and known and appreciated, we will more fully identify with Him and His sacrifice.

This life of love is not meant to earn God's favor; Jesus already did that through His death on the cross. We're not trying to impress God or curry His goodwill. Quite the opposite. It is because of Jesus' great love toward us, filling us, and flowing through us that we live lives of sacrificial love. This isn't an equation of earning; it's a response of gratefulness.

We need to experience God's love in a whole new way, not just so that we can uncover His deep love for us personally, but so that His love would fill us up and overflow into love for everyone, including those hard-to-love people closest to us.

This is exactly what Jesus explained to His disciples the night He was betrayed by one of His own: "Love one another. As I have loved you, so you must love one another. By this everyone will know that you are my disciples, if you love one another" (John 13:34–35). Notice that the definitive marker of a person who belongs to Jesus is not Bible knowledge, it's not evangelistic zeal, and it's not passion for social justice. It's love. In fact, Paul reminds the Corinthian church that even the most sacrificial acts are pointless without love (1 Cor. 13:1–3).

Quite simply, we cannot say that we love Jesus but not actively love our family members, our neighbors, our coworkers, and our enemies. We cannot claim to have experienced Jesus' love and remain indifferent to those suffering around us, or tolerate ancient grudges, or overlook bickering, backbiting, or even mild indifference. Jesus' love compels us to a radical outpouring of love, even to the most unlovable person in our lives.

Picture that person right now . . . the one who always gets on your nerves, whose presence prompts you to leave the room, who makes it hard to look them in the eye. You can't think of anything nice to say about them, but they're your favorite topic of gossip; or you just avoid talking about them altogether. You might not hate them, but if you're totally honest, you feel a grudge simmering below the surface.

Their success makes you feel smaller, and you find yourself secretly cheering when they experience hardship.

Take a moment to write that person's name in the margin.

WHO IS GOD CALLING ME TO LOVE?

Think about that person whose name you wrote in the margin above. Picture them in your mind. What would it look like to love them sacrificially—as Jesus loved His disciples—over the next few weeks?

> Now that I, your Lord and Teacher, have washed your feet, you also should wash one another's feet. I have set you an example that you should do as I have done for you. Very truly I tell you, no servant is greater than his master, nor is a messenger greater than the one who sent him. Now that you know these things, you will be blessed if you do them. (John 13:14–17)

Does loving that person feel uncomfortably hard?

Does it feel belittling to serve them?

Dear friend, I am right there with you.

As I'm writing these words, I am faced with God's call to love two people in my life who have hurt me deeply. We carry baggage from years, even decades, of misunderstandings, missteps, and misgivings. These two people are completely opposite of each other, yet I cannot escape God's clear call to love them in this season of Lent.

By now, you may feel the Spirit's nudge in your heart too. We are called to love . . . not so they will apologize to us. Not so they will see how spiritual we are in loving them even though they've wronged us. But to love them simply so they will experience God's love anew.

Oh, that is so humbling. It's hard. Honestly, it's beyond our own power to love.

But as we die to ourselves and allow Jesus' love to flow through us, we will experience the fellowship of His sufferings, becoming like Him in His death in relationship to these hard-to-love people around us. Good Friday will strike us personally, experientially, like never before, and we'll grow to know the power of Jesus' love not just intellectually, but experientially as we pour ourselves out to love others too. We will uncover Jesus' love toward us and uncover *His love in us* toward others. And as we die to ourselves, we will experience the power of His resurrection like never before (Phil. 3:10–11).

Easter Sunday will gain layers of new meaning as we celebrate

Jesus' victory over death, sin, and evil, not just one time two thousand years ago, but today and every day for all eternity, radiating outward through all time and in all relationships, as His love spills out and into every life we touch.

What might this practice of sacrificial love look like?

I suggest you take some time at the beginning of this Lenten season to ask God how you might love this person He's placed on your heart. I'd venture to guess you already have a few ideas, uncomfortable though they may be. But if you're at a loss for where to start, consider thinking through *The 5 Love Languages* described by Gary Chapman: Words of Affirmation, Quality Time, Gifts, Acts of Service, and Physical Touch.[4] Take out a piece of paper and brainstorm ideas for every category, and commit to one act of sacrificial love every week until Easter Sunday. Even if you don't feel like loving them on any particular day or week, commit to loving obedience—out of your heartfelt love for Jesus, even if not for that particular person. Then allow God to multiply your joy regardless of their response:

> "If you keep my commands, you will remain in my love, just as I have kept my Father's commands and remain in his love. I have told you this so that my joy may be in you and that your joy may be complete." (John 15:10-11)

A PRAYER FOR

YOU AND ME

Heavenly Father, may the eyes of our hearts be enlightened to see Your love toward us, as we never have before. Pour out Your love on us from the fullness of Your glorious and inexhaustible riches, that Christ may dwell in our hearts and strengthen us with power to grasp just how wide and long and high and deep is the love of Christ—so expansive that we can't escape it, so extensive that we can't exhaust it. May we be deeply rooted and established in Your love, growing to know Jesus' love not just in our minds but in our experiences. May Your love fill us to the measure of all the fullness of God, overflowing into the lives of those You have placed in our lives for this very time and purpose. Thank You for doing immeasurably more than we can even imagine right now through Your Spirit's power at work in us, all for Your glory in Jesus Christ for all eternity. Amen. (Prayer based on Eph. 3:16–21.)

WEEK ONE

WEEK ONE CELEBRATION
ASH WEDNESDAY

I f you're going through this devotional with your family, you can visit uncoveringthelove.com, print out the questions and Scripture readings on separate slips of paper, and distribute them among your family members in order to involve everyone. Most of these components are simple enough for even small children to read alone or with help.

OPEN WITH A SIMPLE PRAYER.

LIGHT ALL SEVEN CANDLES ON YOUR LENTEN WREATH, IF USING ONE.

READ THE FOLLOWING VERSES ALOUD:

"When you were dead in your sins and in the uncircumcision of your flesh, God made you alive with Christ. He forgave us all our sins, having canceled the charge of our legal indebtedness, which stood against us and condemned us; he has taken it away, nailing it to the cross." — Colossians 2:13–14

SOMEONE ASKS:

Why did Jesus have to die?

SOMEONE RESPONDS:

Jesus died to forgive us of our sins and cancel our debt.

To symbolize Jesus' death, snuff out one candle on your Lenten wreath, if using one.

Take turns reading through this part of the gospel story:

John 1:1–18

Discussion Questions:

1. Today's text tells us that the law came through Moses; but Jesus brought God's grace and truth and invites us to become God's children. What does this tell us about God?

2. Whenever we break God's law, that's called sin. But Jesus offers us forgiveness through His death on the cross. What sins do you need to confess and ask Him to forgive?

3. What do you want to say in response to Jesus?

Sing the following song together:

"Nothing but the Blood of Jesus" by Robert Lowry (1876)

As you begin reading the daily devotions this week, light all but one of the candles and thank Jesus for the ways He demonstrates His love toward you. After you've finished your daily reading and prayer, blow out the remaining candles.

JESUS LOVES PERFECTLY

*Then Jesus was led by the Spirit into the wilderness
to be tempted by the devil.*

MATTHEW 4:1

Love never fails.

1 CORINTHIANS 13:8

READ THE STORY: MATTHEW 4:1-11

From the first moment of creation, Jesus loved the humans He created. In the garden of Eden, God dwelled with them in perfect harmony. And even when Adam and Eve chose to rebel and disobey, He didn't stop loving them, but promised to redeem humanity and all of creation, so that we may live together again in perfect fellowship for all eternity. But between that promise in the garden and the fulfillment of that promise stretched thousands of years—of wandering, waiting, and wondering when God would come and make His home with humans again.

You likely know many stories of God's people longing for this relationship to be restored and botching attempts to maintain a loving relationship with God in the meantime. Think of Cain and Abel, Abraham and Sarah, Jacob and Esau, Joseph and his brothers. Think of Moses and Joshua, David and Solomon, Isaiah and Jeremiah, and the many priests and kings who tried to lead God's people into a perfect relationship with God.

One failed attempt after another. One dashed hope after another. Who would come to rescue God's people from their sin? Who would restore humankind's relationship with God?

The question hangs in the air, unanswered for one generation after another.

And then Jesus enters the scene. After His public baptism, at the very beginning of Jesus' public ministry on earth, the Spirit of God led Him into the wilderness for forty days of fasting, prayer, and obedience-training. Throughout Scripture, God's servants often faced this kind of extensive testing and preparation before public ministry. Consider Moses's fasting forty days and nights before receiving the law or Elijah's forty-day journey to the mountain of God before encountering Him in the whisper. But mostly, this wilderness experience would have called to the original hearer's mind the Israelites' forty-year wandering: they were in the wilderness because of their disobedience, and they failed test after test.

The tempter challenged Jesus to turn bread into stones, to jump off the temple, and to skip the pain and rejection He would endure by just bowing to him in worship. Jesus was famished, weak from hunger, heat, and thirst, and lonely from isolation. Yet at His most vulnerable point, Jesus declared His continuous trust in His heavenly Father, ending with an exclamation of love for Him:

"Be gone, Satan! For it is written: 'You shall worship the Lord your God and him only shall you serve.'" (Matt. 4:10 ESV)

The hell of hunger and loneliness would not affect Jesus' love, loyalty, and trust in His Father's provision.[1]

Jesus perfectly fulfilled the Father's purpose for His wilderness testing, because where God's people failed to obey God time after time, Jesus demonstrated perfect trust and obedience every time.

And He did it all for love.

With that private victory in the wilderness Jesus launched His public ministry. He had won the first in a series of battles against the enemy of our souls, and He was establishing God's kingdom so that everyone—young and old, poor and rich, sick and healthy, Jewish and pagan—would be welcomed in.

CHALLENGE

As you begin your own forty-day wilderness experience this Lent, take some time to consider: what are your expectations of God?

Of yourself?

Of your experience?

What role do you expect prayer and fasting to take? What questions do you have? What fears or uncertainty are in your heart?

How can you rest in Jesus' perfect obedience rather than trying to muster it up on your own?

Lastly, what does love have to do with your Lenten journey?

End by expressing your thoughts to Jesus in a written prayer, asking Him to help you uncover His perfect love in the weeks to come, helping you more fully accept His love for you and extend His love to others.

PRAYER

Precious Jesus, thank You for the great love with which You have loved me. You have perfectly accomplished what every human has failed to do, and so You've opened the way for me to experience God's perfect love. I confess my fears and uncertainty. Holy Spirit, lead me in my own wilderness journey; teach me perfect love and obedience. Reveal to me Your perfect love for me in Christ Jesus. Amen.

FOR FURTHER STUDY

Exodus 34:27–35; Deuteronomy 8:1–18; 1 Kings 19:1–21;
Matthew 4:1–11; Mark 1:12–13; Luke 4:1–13; John 14:9–31;
Hebrews 4:14–5:10

JESUS INVITES US CLOSE

He appointed twelve that they might be with him.

MARK 3:14

"I have called you friends. . . . Love each other as I have loved you."

JOHN 15:15, 12

READ THE STORY: MARK 3:13-19

F irst-century Israelites were familiar with this model of teacher and disciple. Bright young men who showed promise in their Torah studies could choose to apprentice themselves to a rabbi whose interpretation of the law best matched their own. It was a competitive career field that came with long hours and no pay, but also with the hope that a disciple would someday become a respected rabbi with his own disciples.[2]

But Jesus turned this whole system on its head.

He chose unqualified men—who, according to the customs of the day, had failed to advance in their religious education and instead pursued vocational careers. Far from the model students most rabbis accepted as disciples, these twelve men were ordinary and unremarkable.[3] But Jesus hand-picked each one of them: "You did not choose me, but I chose you" (John 15:16a).

As Creator of the universe, Jesus could have chosen any number of ways to establish His kingdom. Of all the possible options, one-on-one relationships seem to be the most inefficient method, from a pragmatic point of view.

But personal relationships with messy people is the way of love.

Jesus chose these twelve men not just to learn His doctrine but to experience His perfect love, because love changes people. Jesus bestowed on them honor and dignity that exceeded their merit, station, and education, even calling them His friends (John 15:15).

Jesus gathered these twelve men to *be* with Him. Day and night, mile after dusty mile, Jesus poured into them thousands of hours together, doing everything from mundane daily chores to teaching and healing and proclaiming God's kingdom come on earth. Other people only had access to Jesus for a brief moment; a few others traveled with Jesus occasionally; but these twelve got to spend three years of their lives within arm's reach of Jesus.

Yes, through His incarnational ministry on earth, Jesus brought healing and blessing to every person who sincerely sought Him. But to these twelve, Jesus revealed far more than He entrusted to any of His other followers. He invited them behind closed doors to witness private miracles. He explained hard teachings to them. He answered their questions. And He even miraculously provided for them, from calming the angry sea to paying Peter's taxes.

Time with Jesus up close and personal changes us. You cannot spend hours with Love Himself and remain untouched. Even Jesus' opponents recognized this truth, for notice their reaction when Peter and John defend themselves after their arrest: Now when they saw the boldness of Peter and John, and perceived that they were uneducated, common men, they were astonished. And they recognized that they had been with Jesus" (Acts 4:13 ESV). These men had been with Jesus. And it changed everything.

As humans, we are limited by time and space in giving our time to people we love. Being fully human, Jesus also limited this invitation to His twelve disciples during His public ministry on earth. But through His death, resurrection, and ascension to His Father, Jesus invites each of us—His disciples today—to experience the love of His presence through the gift of His Spirit within us, until the coming of that glorious day when He returns and we will see Him face-to-face. Oh what grace! Oh what love!

CHALLENGE

Of all the resources we have been given, time is the most precious. It seems basic to give someone your time and focused attention, but it also feels costly in some ways, doesn't it? To invite someone to share in your life, to see you behind closed doors, and to be your closest friend—that's a precious expression of love. Who is one person you can love in this way today?

PRAYER

Beloved Jesus, thank You for the privilege of being called to You as one of Your own. Thank You for Your Spirit within me, inviting me into fellowship with You. Though I have not seen You, my heart knows You, and I long for the day when I will see You face-to-face. Until then, fill me with the joy of Your presence. Make my heart hunger and thirst to spend time with You. And free me to love others freely with my presence and attention. Forgive me for the times I've been distracted, withholding the gift of my presence from those I love. Help me set aside anything that distracts me and to be fully present with the people You've placed in my life, to love them well. Amen.

FOR FURTHER STUDY

John 1:1–18; 15:9–17; 1 Corinthians 13:12;
Hebrews 4:14–16; 1 John 1:1–4

JESUS DOES NOT BOAST

The master of the banquet tasted the water [Jesus had]
turned into wine. He did not realize where it had come from,
though the servants who had drawn the water knew.

JOHN 2:9

"The Son of Man did not come to be served, but to serve,
and to give his life as a ransom for many."

MATTHEW 20:28

READ THE STORY: JOHN 2

J esus and His disciples had been invited to a wedding, likely that of a close friend or family member. In Jewish culture, wedding celebrations lasted for days and days, even up to a week, and while some guests came and went, others would stay the whole time.

Of paramount importance to a feast is, of course, the food and drink. In a culture that emphasized hospitality, inviting as many guests as possible brought honor to the bridal couple, but running out of food and drink would bring grave shame. However involved Mary was in the food preparations, she was quick to realize they had run out of wine and brings the matter to Jesus' attention.

Much has been made of Jesus' response to His mother, but what's clear is that He's establishing clear boundaries for His ministry: He takes orders from no one but His heavenly Father, and He will act only on His divine timetable. Yet, out of love, Jesus miraculously turns water into wine, saving the groom from public disgrace and humiliation, and also solidifying His disciples' faith in Him. Symbolically, Jesus is ushering in a new era, but few had witnessed the miracle to recognize the importance of the event.

What's fascinating in this narrative is that Jesus doesn't seek public recognition for His first miracle. When the master of ceremony tastes the new wine, he calls the groom aside and remarks on how much better this wine tastes compared to what had first been served. But the text explicitly states that he "did not realize where it had come from, though the servants who had drawn the water knew" (John 2:9). We don't even know if the groom knew where the wine came from. Because that wasn't the point. Not yet. There would be many miraculous signs and wonders to come that would publicly reveal Jesus as the Son of God who has authority over all of creation, yet this first miracle was purposed to reveal His glory to a select few, and also to save His friend from the public embarrassment of running out of fare for his wedding guests.[4]

If anyone had reason to boast, it was Jesus. If anyone would have been justified to make a grand entrance into public ministry with a grand miracle, it was Jesus.

Instead of manipulating people and events to orchestrate a grand entrance into public ministry, Jesus quietly provides for His friends' needs. Jesus didn't seek the spotlight; He didn't chase recognition or applause. He stayed in the shadows, quietly serving and providing, thus setting the tone for His public ministry to come: He had come to serve others, and He would do so at the cost of His very life.

CHALLENGE

Do you struggle with wanting public recognition for the ways you serve others? Do you find your heart longing for praise, likes, and follows? Or are you content to have your acts of love remain anonymous, known only to your heavenly Father and the handful who witness them? Choose someone to encourage or serve today, anonymously if possible, and relish the truth that your act of love is known by God—and that is enough.

PRAYER

Precious Jesus, Your call to humble love is convicting. I confess my desire to be seen and known and recognized. I confess the times I've boasted in my own sacrificial love instead of hiding in Yours. Help me be quick to recognize the needs of those around me, and to serve them without fanfare or expectation of thanks. May Your love fill me to overflowing, and may I bring much joy to You and those You love through me. Amen.

FOR FURTHER STUDY

Matthew 20:20–27; Luke 22:24–30; John 13:12–17;
Philippians 2:5–11

ver wonder how to keep Easter centered on Jesus? The activities below range from hands-on crafts that help you better understand Scripture to new spins on ancient disciplines like fasting, prayer, and almsgiving. They can be used by adults or adapted for children. Pick one or more activities to prepare your heart to celebrate Jesus this Easter.

* **Ask God to reveal your hidden sins,** and write them on slips of paper, confessing each as you write. Acknowledge the gravity of your sins, then burn the papers in a jar and declare Christ's forgiveness over your life (1 John 1:9–10). Crush the ashes and mark ash crosses on your wrists to remember that Jesus bore your sins on the cross. Pour a little oil on a paper towel and wipe the crosses, reading Isaiah 61:1–3. Save the leftover ashes for next year's Ash Wednesday.

* **Create a Lenten candle wreath to use during family devotions.** This can be as simple or as elaborate as you'd like, with a single large pillar candle or seven small votive candles. Find multiple options and tutorials at uncoveringthelove.com.

- **Give up eating at restaurants** for the duration of Lent, opting instead for simple meals like soup and bread. Read Isaiah 58:6–7 and discuss the true fast that God wants from us. Place the money you save in an offering jar to buy grocery store gift cards for families in need.

- **Read through psalms of lament** (Psalms 12, 13, 44, 86) and use them to express to God what grieves your heart right now in your own life and in the world around you. Journal through the hurts you've experienced this past year, and allow our Great Physician to open the wounds and inspect them that He may heal them.

- **Talk to a professional Christian counselor to address deep hurts.** Find someone you trust to walk you through the deep and murky waters of sins committed against you, so that you may learn to forgive and heal and love again. Allow yourself to cry over and mourn the hurt and pain. Sin grieves God, and it can grieve us too.

BONUS CONTENT

Go to uncoveringthelove.com to find step-by-step tutorials, download a free printable activity sheet, and discover other helpful resources to observe Lent together as a family.

WEEK TWO

WEEK TWO CELEBRATION

If you're going through this devotional with your family, you can visit uncoveringthelove.com, print out the questions and Scripture readings on separate slips of paper, and distribute them among your family members in order to involve everyone. Most of these components are simple enough for even small children to read alone or with help.

OPEN WITH A SIMPLE PRAYER.

LIGHT ALL BUT ONE CANDLE ON YOUR LENTEN WREATH, IF USING ONE.

READ THE FOLLOWING VERSE ALOUD:

> "God demonstrates his own love for us in this: While we were still sinners, Christ died for us." — Romans 5:8

SOMEONE ASKS:

> Why did Jesus have to die?

SOMEONE RESPONDS:

> Jesus died to demonstrate His love for us.

SNUFF OUT ANOTHER CANDLE ON YOUR LENTEN WREATH, IF USING ONE.

TAKE TURNS READING THROUGH THIS PART OF THE GOSPEL STORY:

> John 3:14–17

1. How did Jesus demonstrate His love for us?

2. Today's text tells us that when we believe in Jesus, we are saved into eternal life. Have you believed in Jesus for your salvation?

3. What do you want to say in response to Jesus?

SING THE FOLLOWING SONG TOGETHER:

"How Deep the Father's Love for Us" by Stuart Townend (1995)

As you begin reading the daily devotions this week, light all but two of the candles and thank Jesus for the ways He demonstrates His love toward you. After you've finished your daily reading and prayer, blow out the remaining candles.

JESUS CROSSES BORDERS

When a Samaritan woman came to draw water,
Jesus said to her, "Will you give me a drink?"
JOHN 4:7

READ THE STORY: JOHN 4:1-42

n Jesus' day, strict rules defined appropriate behavior between genders, classes, and ethnic groups. Though some originated in the law of Moses, most others had morphed over time to exclude the underdog and insulate the privileged in their own little club.

Interactions between a Jewish man and a Samaritan woman were clearly demarcated: ideally, avoid interaction if at all possible. If unavoidable, minimize contact to avoid becoming ritually unclean.

But in His conversation with the Samaritan woman, Jesus defies these human regulations and shocks even His own disciples.

Jesus intentionally steps into this scene with the Samaritan woman even though political and religious divisions existed between the Jewish people and the Samaritans. Though many Jews traveling between Judea and Galilee chose to take the long route around Samaria, Jesus chose to cross the cultural border into Samaritan territory. Alone at Jacob's well, Jesus sees a lone woman approaching at the hottest hour of the day, and asks her for a drink.

This is problematic for the woman, because most Middle Eastern cultures disapproved of men speaking with women in private, and since Jewish tradition considered Samaritan women continually unclean, drinking from her water jug would make Jesus "impure." The woman challenges Jesus: "How can you ask me for a drink?"

But Jesus knows the heart and love compels Him forward. He invites the woman into a conversation, allowing her to voice her frustration until reaching her predicament: even if she could worship the one true God, where could she worship Him? The Jews had destroyed the Samaritans' holy place, and as a Samaritan woman who had been married five times (which reflected poorly on her character) and was living with a man who wasn't even her husband (shameful by both Jewish and Samaritan standards), she had no hope of worshiping God in His temple in Jerusalem. She was excluded from true worship of God and relegated to a life of quiet desperation, yet her questions reveal a deep longing for God.

Her only hope was to wait for the coming Messiah, the true prophet who followed Moses, who would set all things right. She was burdened by her past choices and trapped by her present circumstances. If only the Messiah would come.

When Jesus asked her to call her husband, she admitted she had no husband, most likely feeling shame because of how often she'd already been married and now she was just living with a man.

Jesus does not rush her for her answer.

He doesn't chastise her.

He doesn't belittle her.

Instead, He does the unthinkable: Jesus reaches across every man-made boundary to quench her deepest longing . . . with Himself. And as if that weren't enough, He honors this Samaritan woman by choosing her to be the first person to whom He reveals His identity as the Messiah: "I am he."

What's more, Jesus chooses her to witness Him not just as Messiah for the Jews, but the Savior of the world. His love truly knows no limits.

CHALLENGE

What stands between you and a joyful relationship with Jesus today? Consider also: What stands between you and a joyful relationship with people He has called you to love, perhaps across social, racial, economic, and cultural borders? Think of the person in your neighborhood who is most unlike you, and prayerfully plan a specific way to show them Jesus' love this week.

PRAYER

Jesus, I praise You for Your love that crossed into my life one day, and every day since then. Thank You that human constraints can't keep Your love out and past sins don't keep Your love away. Thank You for loving me just as I am. Help me love others where they are, and to seek them out with Your great love for them. Amen.

FOR FURTHER STUDY

2 Kings 17:24; Ezra 4:1–24; Luke 9:52–56; Revelation 7:9–12.

JESUS IS KIND

Moved with compassion, Jesus reached out and touched him.
"I am willing," he said. "Be healed!"

MARK 1:41 NLT

There is no fear in love. But perfect love drives out fear.

1 JOHN 4:18

READ THE STORY: MARK 1:29-34

News of Jesus spread quickly throughout the Galilean countryside, and people were flocking to Jesus, bringing their loved ones who were sick and demon-possessed, hoping that finally they would find relief.

And here comes a man with leprosy—an untouchable in Jewish society. No one brought him to Jesus. It's likely he hadn't felt a human touch in years. No hugs after a long day of work. No sympathetic squeeze around the shoulders. No friendly handshakes. After all, anyone who touched a leprous person contracted temporary ritual impurity, which was quite the inconvenience. In addition, to avoid accidental run-ins, leprous people had to yell out, "Unclean! Unclean!" wherever they went.

Can you imagine? The shame, the loneliness, and the isolation must have been devastating.

But this man hears there's a certain Jesus who's been traveling around towns healing people. So he gathers his courage and makes his way toward Jesus, cautiously avoiding contact with the crowd. Jesus is surrounded by people on His left, His right, in front and behind. But finally, the leper sees an opening. Seizing his chance, this man rushes to Jesus and falls on his knees.

"If you are willing, you can make me clean." It's not a request. It's a statement of fact. This man had seen Jesus heal others, and he knew Jesus could do it. But would He want to? Would His kindness extend to a leper? A loner? An unclean outcast?

Hear the fear in his voice.

And then see Jesus' unthinkable generosity that goes beyond what is expected.

A simple word from Jesus could have healed the man. But Jesus saw beyond the man's skin disease into the loneliness of his heart. And He was moved with compassion. Literally, the phrase means His intestines were twisted in response to what He saw.[1] He had a guttural physical reaction to this man's brokenness, and He did the unthinkable: He reached out and touched the man.

The crowds must have gasped.

There are no words to describe what the man must have felt. The warm touch of another human's hand on his skin, the first voluntary contact since his diagnosis, the touch of God Himself.

"I am willing," Jesus said. And He didn't just say it. He showed it. "Be clean!" He exclaimed, and immediately the leprosy left the man and his skin was clean.

Jesus didn't have to do it that way. But His love compelled Him to kindness, to reach beyond the man's body and heal his heart with the kindness of a human's touch.

CHALLENGE

Part of the mystery of Jesus is that God took on human flesh to become man. And in His body, Jesus experienced the full spectrum of human emotion, including pity, indignation, and compassion—all words that describe Jesus' reaction upon seeing His beautiful creation marred by the effects of sin. Yet Jesus didn't just feel emotions in His body, He allowed His emotions to move Him to action, and we now are called to be His hands and feet, showing others His love in incarnate ways. Ask Jesus to help you show love through appropriate touch. Perhaps you could shake the hand of a homeless person, making eye contact and asking their name as you hand them a meal. Or visit someone in a care facility, touching their arm as you speak to them or hand them a thoughtful gift.

PRAYER

Lord Jesus, You showed incredible kindness to this man two thousand years ago, and You continue to shower Your generosity on me through Your Spirit and Your body. I want to be part of that love in action. Take my body, my hands, my arms, and use them today to show Your love toward someone who's wondering today if You're willing to show them kindness and love. Make me part of Your resounding "yes" in someone's life today. Amen.

FOR FURTHER STUDY

Leviticus 13:1–14:32; Isaiah 53:4; Ephesians 4:32

JESUS REJECTS NO ONE

When Jesus saw their faith, he said to the man,
"Take heart, son; your sins are forgiven. . . . Get up,
take up your mat and go home."

MATTHEW 9:2b, 6b

Mercy triumphs over judgment.

JAMES 2:13

READ THE STORY: LUKE 5:17-26

Throughout the Gospels, we see all kinds of people coming to Jesus: some with great faith and some, like today's paralytic man, with great fear.

What is he afraid of? Does he think Jesus will reject him? Interestingly, the gospel writers all note that Jesus saw the friends' faith, not the paralytic man's faith. Unlike others who approached Jesus, this man doesn't even have the courage to believe—he's overcome by fear, knowing the many sins that mar him, possibly believing that his illness was a punishment for some heinous hidden sins.

But his friends insist that this new teacher in town can help him. They love him. They believe even when he doesn't. And when they can't squeeze into the packed house, they carry him to the roof and start hacking at the packed mud and branches to make an opening. With heart pounding, the man sees himself lowered into the crowded room until he's sprawled out right in front of Jesus.

Imagine what you would you feel in his place. Not only are you ruining a neighbor's roof, but your friends interrupt a respected teacher's sermon with your own personal needs. "Umm, excuse us, we know You're important and You're busy, but could You put everything on hold to heal our friend?"

It's audacious. And it's telling, again, that it's not this man's faith but his friends' that Jesus commends.

This courageous cohort was hoping for a miraculous healing, but Jesus doesn't offer them what they're looking for, at least not initially. Jesus will not be obligated or manipulated, even by ingenious efforts. As a hush falls over the crowd, Jesus looks at the man on the mat, glances up at the friends peering through the hole in the ceiling and back down at the man, who is likely trembling with fear.

"Take heart, son," He says (Matt. 9:2). Take heart. Be of good cheer. It's the same phrase Jesus used to calm His disciples on the stormy sea, when He walked toward them and they thought He was a ghost. Jesus cares about the man's fears, and He lovingly starts by addressing those fears. Jesus rejects no one who comes to Him sincerely, though they be fearful.

So Jesus looks at him, recognizes his fear, encourages him, and then pronounces what no one expected: "Your sins are forgiven." That's not what his friends expected, and it's certainly not what the gathered teachers of the law wanted to hear. After all, priests may pronounce God's forgiveness after atonement through a sacrifice, but Jesus was not a Levitical priest, no sacrifice was offered here, and no man assumed the authority to forgive. "Who can forgive sins but God alone?" they fumed in their hearts.

And herein lies Jesus' great love, not just for the paralyzed man on the mat or his friends on the roof above, but for every person standing in that jam-packed room.

So often we want Jesus to manage the effects of sin without actually addressing the root issue. But Jesus loves us too much to offer only a superficial solution. He knows the hidden sins of our hearts, and He lovingly insists on dealing with those first.

So He offers this man forgiveness and offers the crowd a special insight: Jesus is much more than just a miracle-worker; He is God with us.

But some still didn't believe. Words are cheap, they reasoned. Anyone foolish enough to be accused of blasphemy could say what

Jesus said. But to demonstrate His spiritual authority to forgive sins, Jesus pronounces healing; and the man gets up, rolls up his mat, and walks out the door as the crowds who wouldn't let him in part to let him out.

The man walks away with a lightness in his step and praise on his lips, for in one encounter with Jesus, he receives both the healing he wanted but didn't dare hope for and the forgiveness he desperately needed but didn't know to ask for. Jesus altered the course of his life, and he walked home no longer a slave to fear but loudly praising God.

CHALLENGE

Imagine yourself lying on that mat. Who is lowering you through the roof? Which friends in your life demonstrate Jesus' love for you by believing in His compassion and mercy even when you don't dare hope it for yourself? Reach out to those precious friends today and thank them for tangibly demonstrating Jesus' love in your life. Or, perhaps there is a friend who needs to have you "lower them through a roof" to wholeness and healing, either by offering them forgiveness for past hurts, or, if they are physically ill, by offering to make a meal.

PRAYER

Dear Jesus, I confess that sometimes I feel fear when I come to You. I know You love me, but my own heinous sins seem too much, too dark, too evil to bring before You. But You welcome me with open arms and offer forgiveness of all my sins through Your precious blood shed on the cross. Thank You, Jesus, for never rejecting me. Replace my fear with faith, and help me be the kind of friend who helps others encounter You too. Amen.

FOR FURTHER STUDY

Psalms 34:17–20; 94:14; Isaiah 53:3; Matthew 9:1–8; Mark 2:1–12; Luke 5:17–26; John 1:11; James 2:13

JESUS AFFIRMS WHAT IS GOOD

*[Jesus] was amazed at [the centurion], and turning to
the crowd following him, he said, "I tell you, I have not found
such great faith even in Israel."*

LUKE 7:9

READ THE STORY: LUKE 7:1–10

Think of an acquaintance who is least like you. Perhaps someone who's even part of a demographic or institution that has hurt you.

What would it take to see past the hurt and affirm the good in this person?

This is the tension of today's story, because typically Roman centurions were antagonistic toward Jews, and Jews were hostile toward the occupying Romans. The Roman centurion was tasked with keeping the peace in this small town off the Sea of Galilee, and he had military troops at his command who would forcefully and sometimes brutally establish their authority. The Romans feared nothing.

Yet here is a Roman centurion who is unlike the others. The Jewish leaders of Capernaum tell Jesus that this foreigner loves their nation and had even built their synagogue. He was a God-fearing Gentile, but a Gentile nonetheless, and thus ceremonially unclean under Mosaic law.

So when the elders of the town come to Jesus and ask Him to come and heal the centurion's sick servant, they likely expected some resistance from Jesus, because no law-abiding Jew would willingly enter an unclean Gentile's home, let alone a Roman centurion's. Jesus pushes back to test their hearts, but they plead with Him: this Roman built their synagogue, and they didn't want to lose his good favor, even if it meant compromising their purity laws on this point. Quite possibly, Jesus is revealing the duplicity of their hearts, as these religious teachers condemned Jesus for healing on the Sabbath but were now asking Him to bend the rules for their own self-interest.

Nonetheless, Jesus sets out toward the centurion's home. He was nearly there when He was met by the friends the centurion had sent to deliver his message: "Lord, don't trouble yourself, for I do not deserve to have you come under my roof." The centurion understood Jewish purity laws well enough to know that Jesus would be defiling Himself by entering his home. And though he was a man in authority, his humility shines bright. The message from the centurion continued: "That is why I did not even consider myself worthy to come to you. But say the word, and my servant will be healed."

Amidst the elders' pleading, the centurion's humility and faith stand in stark contrast. He commanded the respect of his troops and the people, yet he recognized that he didn't deserve Jesus' intervention or even His presence. Recognizing his own unworthiness in the presence of such divine power, he asked for what he didn't deserve with an unparalleled faith.

And Jesus was amazed.

The elders saw only the centurion's outward appearance, his position of power, his potential to help them with their own needs. Jesus saw this man's past, his hurts, his accomplishments, his disappointments, and his willful choice to believe Jesus was who He said He was, even though he'd never met Him.

Jesus saw his faith, and He loved what He saw.

The pioneer and perfecter of our faith (Heb. 12:2) recognized the seeds of belief blooming into unwavering trust, and He marveled at the man. It wasn't a rabbi, or a disciple, or a scribe or a synagogue elder that impressed Jesus. It was a Roman soldier.

Jesus breaks through cultural boundaries by affirming the good in this foreigner and proclaiming God's plan to welcome all His children from around the world into His kingdom; yet those Jews who resisted Him would be thrown out (see Matt. 8:11–12).

When it comes to faith in Jesus, it's not enough to inherit a religion from your parents or to follow a set of rules. Faith in Jesus must be personal and sincere, though it be small. A little, in Jesus' hands, is enough.

CHALLENGE

Jesus is quick to acclaim faith and reward those who seek Him. Think back on the past week. Where is there evidence of faith in Jesus in your life? Where did you try to figure things out on your own? Choose a situation or a relationship that is challenging you right now, and ask Jesus to do what only He can do in and through you. Then watch Him work miracles for His glory and your good.

PRAYER

Dear Jesus, You are in charge of every molecule in the universe, but so often I try to solve my own problems instead of turning to You. Forgive me. Help me believe You, to trust You with the big and small of my everyday life. Thank You for loving me and for championing the good You see, even when it's small. Continue growing my faith, and help me champion the good I see in others too. Amen.

FOR FURTHER STUDY

1 Samuel 16:7; Matthew 8:5–13; Hebrews 12:2

JESUS PAYS ATTENTION

When the Lord saw her, his heart went out to her
and he said, "Don't cry." Then he went up and touched the bier
they were carrying him on. . . . He said, "Young man, I say to you,
get up!" The dead man sat up and began to talk,
and Jesus gave him back to his mother.

LUKE 7:13–15

READ THE STORY: LUKE 7:11-17

Those of us who have grown up around the church often take for granted Jesus' power over life and resurrection. It's what we celebrate at Easter, and what we take comfort in when our own loved ones pass away, grieving but with the hope of seeing them again.

But for people in Jesus' day, death had a finality that was hard to shake; though some believed in the resurrection, others did not. And in any case, dying without an heir to carry on one's name was considered an especially shameful punishment from God and would render a woman completely helpless, likely thrusting her into a life of poverty and obscurity.

It's within this context that, early in His ministry, Jesus encounters a funeral procession as He approaches a small town just south of Nazareth where He had grown up. Such a view would have been familiar to Jesus, though nonetheless heartbreaking. Death is an atrocious affront to God's original design for life and vitality on earth.

But especially sorrowful was the grieving mother's state: now a childless widow, this woman had no one to provide for her in her old age, and would need to cast herself on the mercy of relatives. There was no bright future for her, only dread for eking out a living until death brought relief from her miserable existence.

Jesus knew this. He paid attention. And His compassion moved Him . . . not to join them in their weeping but to do something about it. Caring for widows and orphans is a major theme in both the Old and New Testaments, a demonstration of true love for God by paying attention to the needs of the vulnerable.

"When the Lord saw her face, his heart went out to her" (Luke 7:13). But He didn't step out of the way of the funeral procession. He didn't just make a mental note of the situation and say a little prayer for comfort. He allowed the grief and devastation to affect Him deep within, causing a guttural response of affection.[2] Jesus had likely encountered weeping women before and would do so many times more, but His compassion was fresh as He entered into this woman's story to rewrite the ending. Reaching her, Jesus said, "Don't cry," not because her grief was unwarranted, but because He was joining her in her grief to turn her mourning into gladness.

No one that day expected a miracle. There had been no resurrection for hundreds of years, and over the course of history, only two young men had been restored to their mothers. This grieving mother had no reason to hope for a miracle.

But when Jesus walks onto the scene, there is always hope of a miracle. Because Jesus sees. He notices the details. And He cares.

Jesus simply speaks, and life immediately fills the boy's body. And the people recognize God's power at work in Jesus, exclaiming that God has visited His people.

After hundreds of years of silence, God had sent another prophet, and His miracles attested to His divine power. But the people didn't quite understand the magnitude of Jesus' mission or the way His love would lead Him to the ultimate sacrifice.

CHALLENGE

Rather than offer empty words, Jesus moves swiftly to action. Look around you. Where is there suffering and pain? How might Christ's compassion within you move you to action? Prayerfully consider one practical way you may help alleviate someone's pain, and ask God to multiply your efforts as only He can do.

PRAYER

O Jesus, You are the Giver of Life. You speak, and the universe obeys. And yet You see and care about the smallest details of my life. Nothing escapes Your notice. Though You have every right to be aloof from Your kingdom, instead You choose to be present with Your people and sensitive to our pain. Thank You for placing Your Spirit within me, for grieving with me in my suffering, for caring enough to see, to know, and to care. Help me do the same for the people around me today. Help me enter their suffering, carry their burdens, and bring the hope of Your presence. Amen.

FOR FURTHER STUDY

1 Kings 17:17–24; 2 Kings 4:32–37; Romans 12:15;
Galatians 6:2; James 1:27

*E*ver wonder how to keep Easter centered on Jesus? The activities below range from hands-on crafts that help you better understand Scripture to new spins on ancient disciplines like fasting, prayer, and almsgiving. They can be used by adults or adapted for children. Pick one or more activities to prepare your heart to celebrate Jesus this Easter.

* **Memorize John 3:16,** reciting it in the car, at mealtimes, and at bedtime. Write it on sticky notes, personalizing with the words "God so loved YOU that He gave . . ." Leave in random places (like public restrooms, park benches, Laundromats) as a reminder of Jesus' great love for all.

* **Fill a simple jar with prayer requests** on pieces of paper or craft sticks. Designate a day of the week as your special prayer day, and spend time praying through one or more of the requests. These can be general requests (like orphans, widows, missionaries, government leaders, etc.) or specific requests (like the names of friends and family who are unsaved, sick, deployed, or going through hardship).

✳ **Plant a resurrection garden.** Lay a small clay pot on its side in the center of a large dish and then cover the pot's sides and top with dirt, leaving the opening visible. Plant grass seeds and decorate with rocks, twigs, moss, and other items of your choice. Place your resurrection garden in a sunny spot next to a window and water lightly with a spray bottle each day. During Holy Week, craft three small crosses out of twigs and plant on top of the "hill." Cover the pot opening with a large stone on Good Friday, and then roll it away on Resurrection Sunday, filling the pot opening with fresh flowers.

✳ **Craft a Passover lamb** for your Lenten station. Print out an image of a lamb and use it as a template to cut from cardboard. Wrap white yarn around the cardboard lamb and secure it tightly. Read Exodus 12:1–13 and discuss how Jesus demonstrated His love by becoming the Lamb of God who took away the sins of the world.

✳ **Create a Lenten station** to store your crafts throughout the Lent season. I set out a simple tray in the kitchen and add our Ash Wednesday jar, prayer jar, offering jar, crowns of righteousness, Passover lambs, and other crafts as we make them. Try doing this. Then throughout the week, pick up one of the objects and use it as a prompt to retell the story of Jesus.

BONUS CONTENT

Go to uncoveringthelove.com to find step-by-step tutorials, download a free printable activity sheet, and discover other helpful resources to observe Lent together as a family.

WEEK THREE

I f you're going through this devotional with your family, you can visit uncoveringthelove.com, print out the questions and Scripture readings on separate slips of paper, and distribute them among your family members in order to involve everyone. Most of these components are simple enough for even small children to read alone or with help.

OPEN WITH A SIMPLE PRAYER.

LIGHT ALL BUT TWO CANDLES ON YOUR LENTEN WREATH, IF USING ONE.

READ THE FOLLOWING VERSE ALOUD:

> "In him and through faith in him we may approach God with freedom and confidence." — Ephesians 3:12

SOMEONE ASKS:

> Why did Jesus have to die?

SOMEONE RESPONDS:

> Jesus died that we may worship God freely and confidently in His presence.

SNUFF OUT ANOTHER CANDLE ON YOUR LENTEN WREATH, IF USING ONE.

TAKE TURNS READING THROUGH THIS PART OF THE GOSPEL STORY:

> John 4:7–26

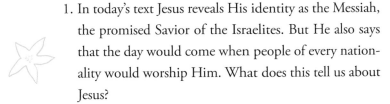

1. In today's text Jesus reveals His identity as the Messiah, the promised Savior of the Israelites. But He also says that the day would come when people of every nationality would worship Him. What does this tell us about Jesus?

2. In Jesus' day, it would have been unusual for a Jewish man to talk to a woman who was considered sinful. How does this conversation demonstrate Jesus' love for her? For you?

3. What do you want to say in response to Jesus?

Sing the following song together:

"When I Survey the Wondrous Cross" by Isaac Watts (1707)

As you begin reading the daily devotions this week, light all but three of the candles and thank Jesus for the ways He demonstrates His love toward you. After you've finished your daily reading and prayer, blow out the remaining candles.

JESUS HONORS THE DISHONORED

"Do you see this woman? . . . her many sins have been forgiven—as her great love has shown."

LUKE 7:44, 47

Love . . . does not dishonor others.

1 CORINTHIANS 13:5

READ THE STORY: LUKE 7:36-50

Jesus was constantly upsetting the teachers of the law, hanging out with the wrong crowds and showing little regard for their additional regulations added to Moses's law. But one night, Jesus was dining in a Pharisee's house. Things seem to be going well.

Until a "sinful woman" walks in and lavishes her love and worship on Jesus, weeping over His feet (how emotional!), wiping the smudgy dust with her own hair (how immodest!), kissing His feet (how preposterous!), and pouring her expensive perfume on them (how wasteful!). The whole scene disrupts Simon's dinner party. Not only is this woman sinful, she's uninvited, and her actions are distracting. Everyone around the low tables sees her, hears her, smells her.

And Simon grows resentful, mentally criticizing Jesus. *If He's truly a prophet, He knows what kind of a woman she is and would rebuke her shameful behavior, dismissing her with scorn.*

But Jesus displays His prophetic powers differently, discerning Simon's thoughts and telling him a story that reveals the depths of His love: Two people owed money—one ten times more than the other—and both were forgiven their debts. Who would love their forgiver more?

Through this parable, Jesus extends forgiveness to both characters at the table. Both Simon and the sinful woman have equal access to the cascade of love flowing from Jesus.

The parched one drinks deeply and exudes loving gratitude. The content one takes a sip and turns away. Jesus offered His love and forgiveness to both that night, but only one received and was transformed.

In ancient times, all good hosts would have greeted their guests with a kiss and supplied water for their guests to wash their feet (or asked a servant to do the task for them). For honored guests, like Jesus, the host would also provide olive oil to anoint their heads out of extreme respect. But whether out of negligence or intentional rudeness, Simon did not offer Jesus these basic courtesies. And Jesus, ignoring normal protocols in an honor-shame culture, openly exposes Simon's inhospitality, contrasting his stinginess with the woman's lavishness.

Why did Simon invite Jesus in the first place, if not out of love?

Perhaps it was to save face. Inviting a traveling teacher into one's home, and even throwing a banquet in his honor, would have been considered the virtuous thing to do. His neighbors would have commended Simon for a job well done, but Jesus sees through the veneer and cuts to the heart: showing Simon that it comes down to love.

Jesus freely pours out His love on all, but only those aware of their sins receive His gift and cling to Him for life.

In ordinary conditions, Simon would have not feared comparison with the sinful woman. He outperformed her in every letter of the law. Except one, Jesus points out. The most important one. Love. Because "whoever has been forgiven little loves little." But love encapsulates the entirety of the law.

Jesus didn't debate the woman's condition with Simon; they all knew she was a sinner. But He transformed her identity from atrocious sinner to acceptable worshiper. Turning to speak to her, Jesus offers her the greatest gift: a new relationship with the almighty God through the forgiveness of all her sins.

Don't miss Jesus' dramatic statement here—the dinner guests didn't. Only priests could pronounce God's forgiveness—and only after appropriate sacrifices had been offered and accepted in the temple courts. But only God Himself could forgive sins. And here, Jesus was stepping into that role, declaring, in effect, God's presence in that very room, extending forgiveness, reconciliation, and a fresh start to the most unlikely recipient.

CHALLENGE

Many of us, like the Pharisee in this story, hide behind false personas, a self-protection mechanism that we can use in our relationships with others and with God too. But Jesus does not look at the outward appearance—He looks at the heart, His gaze penetrating the external actions of righteousness straight to the secret motivations of the heart. Does that frighten you? Comfort you? Respond to Jesus' words of forgiveness not as you feel you should, but as you really feel inside. He knows your thoughts anyway. Lay them bare before Him.

PRAYER

Precious Jesus, You created me in my mother's womb, and you know my secret thoughts. How wonderful is Your love for me! Forgive me for those times when I go through the motions of a relationship without love. Stir in me a sincere love for You that consumes all other thoughts and motives. Forgive me also for judging others by my own standards; help me see others through Your eyes. You have loved me much, and You forgive me much. Help me love You more. Amen.

FOR FURTHER STUDY

1 Samuel 16:7; Psalm 139; Matthew 22:36–40;
Luke 5:30–32; 7:36–50; 1 Corinthians 8:3; 13:12

JESUS SEES FULLY

He said to her, "Daughter, your faith has healed you.
Go in peace and be freed from your suffering."

MARK 5:34

I am fully known.

1 CORINTHIANS 13:12b

READ THE STORY: MARK 5:25-34

A s Jesus was on His way to heal a little girl, He was interrupted by the touch of an anonymous woman. But this wasn't just any woman—she was suffering from an illness that rendered her ceremonially "unclean" according to Levitical law. Anything she touched became unclean, so we can imagine how hard she would have searched for a cure. In fact, Scripture tells us she had spent all her money pursuing medical care, only to worsen instead of experiencing relief.

God intended these Levitical laws to impress on the Israelites' hearts His utter holiness and their lack of holiness. Everyone would have experienced biological uncleanliness from time to time, underscoring their need for purification to approach a holy God. This makes sense as an object lesson, but the woman in this story leverages her invisibility for a shot at touching the fringe of Jesus' garment. Such an act was not just unlawful—it was brazen.

The moment she touches Jesus—immediately—she is healed. She literally feels free from her suffering. And for a moment, she marvels at the miracle. After years of suffering, she is finally whole and healthy!

Well, not quite. Because although her body was healed, her spirit is still broken. Her identity has been shaped by years of disappointment, loneliness, and shunning. She was a nobody to everybody, but to Jesus she is somebody.

"Who touched my clothes?" He wants to know. On a merely human level, the woman's touch would have rendered Jesus unclean. But Jesus is not defiled by the woman's touch; He who created the ceremonial laws defines what is clean. But the woman didn't know that.

Not surprisingly, the woman hangs back, clinging to her invisibility like a security blanket. If she's discovered, she risks public shaming and ridicule. We can imagine she presses back into the crowd, staring at the ground to avoid detection. But Jesus pursues her. He keeps looking around to see who has done it, not because He doesn't already know, but because He wants to offer her more than just physical healing.

"Seeing that she could not go unnoticed," Luke 8:47 says, the woman falls to His feet, trembling with trepidation, and tells what she did and why. The crowd waits with bated breath.

"Daughter," Jesus says. *Daughter.* This woman who had been suffering invisibility and isolation for twelve years hears a term of endearment reserved for one's own family member. This is the only time Jesus directly addresses someone as daughter, and this one single word bestows the mantle of dignity upon this woman's frail shoulders. His words prompt her to lift her gaze from the ground to discover the most surprising gift of all: belonging.

"Daughter, your faith has healed you. Go in peace and be freed from your suffering" (Mark 5:34). Rather than rebuke her boldness, Jesus commends her faith and releases her of any culpability, blessing her with peace, and restoring not just her health but her identity, her dignity, and her visibility.

This is the love of Jesus—a love that pursues, a love that sees, and a love that offers the gift of being seen. We don't have to hide anymore. Let us step up to Him and receive His gift of belonging to Him.

CHALLENGE

Since the garden of Eden, humans have been adept at hiding from God in our shame and sorrow. What areas of your life are you trying to hide from God? Today, Jesus invites you into His presence to discover healing and belonging. Like the woman in today's reading, make your way to Jesus and allow Him to bring healing and restoration to those broken places.

PRAYER

Lord Jesus, You are the God who sees, who knows, and who cares. Nothing escapes Your notice; no pain too insignificant; no hurt too obscure. Thank You that You make time for the unimportant people in this world . . . that You make time for me and that You welcome all to come and find our place of belonging with You. You know me fully, and You love me anyway. I'm so grateful for You. I love You, Lord. Amen.

FOR FURTHER STUDY

Leviticus 15:25–30; Matthew 9:20–22; Luke 8:43–48

JESUS DOES NOT ENVY

*When Jesus landed and saw a large crowd, he had compassion
on them, because they were like sheep without a shepherd. . . .
Then Jesus directed them to have all the people sit down in groups
on the green grass. . . . They all ate and were satisfied.*

MARK 6:34, 39, 42

*Jesus, knowing that they intended to come and make him king
by force, withdrew again to a mountain by himself.*

JOHN 6:15

READ THE STORY: MARK 6:7-44

As Jesus traveled the countryside proclaiming God's coming kingdom, healing the sick, and loving the unlovable, He attracted crowds who were desperate for change. But Jesus was a King without a throne, a Messiah without an army, and a disappointment to those hoping for a Jewish savior to overthrow Roman opposition.

Because when they tried to force Jesus to become king, He disappeared.

Here was a man finally worthy of ruling over the Jewish people, and He refused their political agenda. What a letdown!

For a bit of context, think of their current rulers: Herod called himself the king of the Jews but abused his power, levying heavy taxes to construct three palaces, throwing lavish banquets when his people hungered, and silencing righteous men who spoke against him. Far from shepherding the Israelites, Herod preyed on them.

And the priests, Pharisees, and teachers of the law were no better. Jesus rebukes them for laying heavy burdens on the people that they themselves could not keep. They kept the letter of the law but neglected the weak and oppressed. They taught God's law but hindered those who were seeking Him (see Luke 11:37–54).

All these men were supposed to be shepherding the sheep of Israel, but Jesus looks toward the crowds and sees sheep without a shepherd.

That's not normal.

Sheep without a shepherd quickly get into trouble. They wander into dangerous territory rife with predators. They starve for lack of green pastures. They get scratched and bruised and die alone. And that was the desperate state of the Jewish people at this time.

The shepherds God had given the Israelites were failing their assignment, but God promised to send a shepherd king like David, who would tend the people, bind up the injured, strengthen the weak, and feed them in green pastures (see Ezek. 34).[1]

It's within this larger narrative that Jesus has compassion on the crowds. They're desperate—He leads them. They're sick—He heals them. They're hungry—He sits them in the green grass on the hill to feed them. His fulfillment of the shepherd king prophecy is so obvious that the crowds want to make Him king by force.

But Jesus was focused on the mission His Father had given Him. He rested in the timing His Father ordained, and He refused to grasp for a good thing in the wrong way. Jesus would indeed become their king, but only in God's timing and in the most *unenviable* way.

Jesus didn't love the people because of what they could offer Him. He didn't show off His divine power to garner support for a military coup. He saw a need, and being moved with compassion, He did what every good shepherd does: He took care of His sheep—a free gift, with no strings attached.

CHALLENGE

Envy and love cannot dwell in the same heart, because one is self-promoting and the other is self-giving. Envy makes us feel sorry for ourselves; love compels us to give ourselves. Envy causes us to sacrifice others' good; love causes us to sacrifice ourselves for others' good. How has envy robbed you of the opportunity to love?

PRAYER

Good Shepherd, I would be lost without You. Thank You for loving and serving me even though You deserve all my love and all my service. Forgive me for being envious of others who seem to have the things I want. Help me instead cling to You and find my joy and satisfaction in You alone. Make me a servant of those around me, and pour out Your blessings through me richly. Amen.

FOR FURTHER STUDY

1 Kings 22:17; 2 Kings 4:42–44; Psalms 23; 37:1–11; 73; Ezekiel 34:5, 23–25; John 10:1–21; Revelation 7:17

JESUS DRIVES OUT FEAR

"Take courage! It is I. Don't be afraid."

MATTHEW 14:27

There is no fear in love. But perfect love drives out fear.

1 JOHN 4:18

READ THE STORY: MATTHEW 14:22-33

The disciples had no reason to expect Jesus to walk on the stormy water toward their fishing boat. As far as the disciples knew, Jesus had sent them off to the other side of the lake while He stayed behind to pray on the mountainside, as was His custom. They likely didn't expect to see Him until later the next day, when He'd be able to catch a ride across the lake. He hadn't given them any indication that He was going to meet them at sea. So when they see a person walking on water, they understandably conclude it is either a ghost or an angel.[2]

Jesus anticipated their reaction. After all, He had seen them from the mountainside, being tossed about by the waves. He could have calmed the sea from His spot on the mountainside. He could have miraculously sped the boat to shore (as we find out, He in fact did, upon entering the boat; see John 6:21). But He chose this very method of appearing to them, knowing full well how they would react. It's not surprising, then, that His first words to them are, "Take courage! It is I. Don't be afraid." They were, after all, quite afraid. But Jesus' greeting doesn't just mean "It's Me, Jesus." Jesus is making a very clear identity claim to be God in flesh, taking on God's name as He had revealed Himself to Moses: I am.[3]

This revelation explains Peter's enthusiasm to walk on water, especially within the broader context of Scripture. After all, Moses had demonstrated God's deliverance by leading the people across the Red Sea, and Joshua likewise led the people across the flooded Jordan at God's command. So Peter demonstrates his faith in Jesus by asking to participate in this miraculous moment of divine revelation; he wants Jesus to command him to walk toward Him on stormy waters.

This act of faith tests Peter's trust in Jesus, but also offers to reinforce the disciples' belief in Jesus' God-claim. If Jesus really is who He says He is, then He will do what only He can do.

There is Peter, rocking on his feet as the waves soak his robe, awaiting Jesus' command. Then Jesus commands calmly, confidently: "Come."

Peter climbs out of the boat, one tentative step in front of the other, the sloshing waves becoming like packed dirt under the soles of his sandals. Adrenaline pumping through his veins, he keeps walking toward Jesus. Incredible! Truly this Man is who He says He is! Imagine, as Peter's eyes lock on Jesus, and he shakes his head incredulously. This is really happening!

But out of the corner of his eye, Peter sees the violent winds whipping up the waves; the physical circumstances threaten his burgeoning faith. Faith turns to fear as the water turns liquid under his feet. Peter begins sinking. Death is imminent. "Lord, save me!" he cries out.

Immediately, Jesus reaches out. "You of little faith," Jesus says, as He hoists him out of the water. "Why did you doubt?" The water becomes solid under their feet as they walk back to the boat.[4]

Even after Peter's sinking faith, Jesus offers him the once-in-a-lifetime opportunity to walk on water—this time not toward Jesus, but alongside Him, free of fear because of Love Himself.

The apostle John picks up this motif in his verses to believers: "In this world, we are like Jesus. There is no fear in love. But perfect love drives out fear, because fear has to do with punishment. The one who fears is not made perfect in love. We love because he first loved us" (1 John 4:17b–19).

Jesus doesn't require steadfast faith to ensure His steadfast love. He continues to love despite our failings and our doubts because Jesus' perfect love drives out fear.

CHALLENGE

In your own life, how has Jesus revealed both His divinity and His love toward you? Are there any sinking moments in your life that have caused you to doubt Jesus' love for you? What would it look like to grasp Jesus' outstretched arm and allow Him to walk you back to the boat? Also, who do you know who might be doubting the love and trustworthiness of Jesus right now? Take a few moments to pray for them.

PRAYER

Creator God, You are the One who spoke this world into existence. You're the same One who spoke peace over the storm that night and the One who commands the storms in my life. Forgive me for doubting Your power and Your love. I'm so grateful that Your love for me is not dependent on my faith in You. Continue to drive out any speck of fear in my heart. Help me trust You wholeheartedly and step out in faith when You call me to walk with You. Amen.

FOR FURTHER STUDY

Exodus 14–15; Joshua 3:1–16; Isaiah 41:10; 43:1–2;
John 6:16–21; 1 John 4:11–19

JESUS LOVES INDISCRIMINATELY

"Woman, you have great faith! Your request is granted."

MATTHEW 15:28

READ THE STORY: MATTHEW 15:21-28

Matthew sets the stage for Jesus' exchange with this Canaanite woman, following a rather frustrating exchange between Jesus and the teachers of the law, who were stuck on ceremonial purity laws and were missing the main point: that it was an inner heart of faith in God that rendered one acceptable before Him, not an outward claim of religiosity or nationality.

Jesus shakes the dust off His feet, so to speak, and leaves Israelite territory for a jaunt into Gentile lands, heading on a forty-mile journey northwest toward the Mediterranean coast in the region of Tyre and Sidon, the epitome of Gentile "uncleanness." His disciples would have been uneasy in this place, as Canaanite descendants were abhorred by the Jews. After all, these were the great-great-grandchildren of those idolatrous nations Israel was supposed to exterminate once they entered the promised land. They had likely been pushed north, out of Israelite territory, but still close enough to have enticed God's people toward despicable idolatrous practices. Any serious law-abiding Jew would have avoided this area, yet Jesus headed straight into it.

The journey would have taken days, giving Jesus and His disciples plenty of time to talk. It's possible that on the way to these cities, the disciples would have thought of another man of God who traveled this same route. Elijah took up residence with a Canaanite woman while eluding the wicked Israelite king during the famine in Israel. God had miraculously multiplied her flour and oil for the duration of the drought, and through Elijah's intercession even raised her son from the dead. There was precedent for what Jesus was doing here; when Israel rejected God's rightful reign, the Gentile nations could experience His undeserving grace in their stead.

Somewhere on this journey into foreign territory, a Canaanite woman pursues Jesus, desperately crying out for mercy: "Lord, Son of David have mercy on me! My daughter is demon-possessed and suffering terribly." Yet Jesus says nothing. He doesn't even seem to acknowledge her.

Undeterred, the woman follows Him, continuing her pleas and

annoying the disciples. Finally, they'd had enough. "Send her away," they demand, "for she keeps crying out after us." This woman would not give up.

Jesus turns to face her and gives her a good reason He shouldn't honor her request: He was sent not to the Gentiles but to the lost sheep of Israel. Though this woman's religious knowledge was limited, she surely knew that God had made a promise to Abraham, Isaac, and Israel, not to the descendants of Canaan. She had no claim on Him.

But she falls at His feet, placing herself under His authority and lordship, asking again for His help. Still Jesus does not give in. Doesn't she know the children's food shouldn't be tossed to dogs?

Notice Jesus' willingness to engage in conversation with this woman. It seems Jesus is not rebuking her as much as testing the persistence of her faith; whether for her benefit or His disciples, we do not know. Would she turn around and leave, dejected? Would she pridefully spit on His feet, taking offense at the perceived insult? Or would she persist in her faith?

The woman humbles herself even more; she doesn't contradict Jesus, but cleverly builds on His argument: even dogs eat the crumbs on the floor. From her very first cry (acknowledging Jesus as the rightful King of Israel) to this poignant moment at His feet, (calling on the compassion of God), this Canaanite woman shows more faith, maturity, and humility than the Pharisees and teachers of the law who Jesus had offended earlier in the chapter. This woman was desperate for her darling daughter, she was confident in Jesus' power and reign, and she wasn't going anywhere until she got what she pleaded for, even if she didn't deserve it.

Jesus wastes no time, enthusiastically affirming her faith, commending her above the Pharisees and teachers of the law: "Woman, you have great faith! Your request is granted!" And instantly her daughter was healed. She had received what she had tenaciously pursued, but Jesus offered her much more, commending her faith above that of His own people, as He had with the Gentile centurion (see Matt. 8:13).

The very people Jesus had come to save were rejecting Him, yet here in Gentile territory Jesus found mature and humble faith that deeply touched Him, signaling the beginning of the expansion of His rule and kingdom's reign over all people everywhere, the fulfillment of His promise to Abraham that through Him all nations would be blessed.

CHALLENGE

Often Jesus seems to postpone an immediate reply to our requests, either to reveal the sincerity of our own hearts or to reveal Himself in some other ways to those watching. Yet make no mistake—His character is love and His purpose is always for our good. Have you ever found yourself frustrated by Jesus' apparent delay to answer your prayers? How might His silence in your life actually be a sign of love?

PRAYER

King Jesus, You alone reign as the Son of David on Your throne. Your kingdom come, Your will be done, on earth and in my life as it is in heaven. Forgive me for often becoming impatient with Your timing. I don't understand, but I want to have faith like this woman. Help me cling to what I know is true about Your love and character when I find myself frustrated with Your unresponsiveness. Grow me in my understanding of Your love for me and for those around me. Amen.

FOR FURTHER STUDY

1 Kings 17:7–24; Matthew 8:5–13; 15:21–28; Mark 7:24–30;
John 1:11–12

*E*ver wonder how to keep Easter centered on Jesus? The activities below range from hands-on crafts that help you better understand Scripture to new spins on ancient disciplines like fasting, prayer, and almsgiving. They can be used by adults or adapted for children. Pick one or more activities to prepare your heart to celebrate Jesus this Easter.

* **Deliver a bouquet of flowers** to someone who has lost a loved one this past year, and pray for them specifically this week.

* **Memorize a longer passage of Scripture** together, learning a verse a week (great ones to start with are Isaiah 53, John 19, Philippians 2, or 1 Corinthians 13). Take turns saying a verse around the dinner table, or make up signs to go with the verses. Find more memorizing tips and techniques on the website.

* **Watch a video adaptation of Jesus' life** and discuss how well it represents the gospel narrative.

* **Make a resurrection set** (like a nativity set, but for Easter) and display it in a prominent place where you can discuss Jesus' story throughout Lent.

✳ **Create a Lenten playlist** filled with sacred songs that point your heart and mind to Jesus, and fast from your typical music selection. Or listen to the *Lent: Uncovering the Love of Jesus* playlist on Spotify, featuring my family's favorite songs for the Lenten season.

BONUS CONTENT

 Go to uncoveringthelove.com to find our favorite videos, a free printable activity sheet, and other helpful resources to observe Lent together as a family.

WEEK FOUR

WEEK FOUR CELEBRATION

I f you're going through this devotional with your family, you can visit uncoveringthelove.com, print out the questions and Scripture readings on separate slips of paper, and distribute them among your family members in order to involve everyone. Most of these components are simple enough for even small children to read alone or with help.

OPEN WITH A SIMPLE PRAYER.

LIGHT ALL BUT THREE CANDLES ON YOUR LENTEN WREATH, IF USING ONE.

READ THE FOLLOWING VERSE ALOUD:

> "For the wages of sin is death, but the gift of God is eternal life in Christ Jesus our Lord." — Romans 6:23

SOMEONE ASKS:

> Why did Jesus have to die?

SOMEONE RESPONDS:

> Jesus died to give us eternal life with Him.

SNUFF OUT ANOTHER CANDLE ON YOUR LENTEN WREATH, IF USING ONE.

TAKE TURNS READING THROUGH THIS PART OF THE GOSPEL STORY:

> John 6:35–40

1. Jesus says that God's will is that everyone who believes in Him will have eternal life. What does this tell us about God?

2. What do you want to say in response to Jesus?

3. How might you share this good news with others who need to hear it today?

Sing the following song together:

"The Old Rugged Cross" by George Bennard (1913)

As you begin reading the daily devotions this week, light the last three candles and thank Jesus for the ways He demonstrates His love toward you. After you've finished your daily reading and prayer, blow out the remaining candles.

JESUS LOVES THE LEAST OF THESE

People were bringing little children to Jesus for him
to place his hands on them, but the disciples rebuked them.
When Jesus saw this, he was indignant. He said to them,
"Let the little children come to me, and do not hinder them,
for the kingdom of God belongs to such as these."

MARK 10:13–14

"If you love those who love you, what reward will you get?"

MATTHEW 5:46a

READ THE STORY: MARK 10:13-16

In today's social media–driven culture, we're used to name-dropping, endorsing, tagging, and self-promotion. I once heard an influencer boldly declare from the stage, "It's not about who you know, it's about who knows you."

And while that kind of worldly wisdom may help some people land book deals or job referrals, the kingdom of God reveals an upside-down economics. Or rather, it provides a right-side-up perspective to our world's upside-down mentality.

There's a grain of truth in that speaker's networking advice, but I imagine it's not quite what he had in mind. After all, what's important truly is Who knows you, with a capital "W." There will be many on the final judgment day who will hear those frightful words from Jesus: "I never knew you. Away from me, you evildoers!" (Matt. 7:23)

But if you know Jesus and Jesus knows you, it doesn't matter how well-known or unknown you are to the rest of the world. You can rest in His intimate and unconditional love. He is enough.

We see this time and time again in Jesus, in the way He reached out to those shoved aside by power-mongers and in the way He taught His disciples to do the same, serving meals to the hungry, offering hospitality to the foreigner, visiting the sick and imprisoned. Jesus was stretching His followers' understanding of what God's kingdom of love looked like, even going so far as to teach: "When you give a banquet, invite the poor, the crippled, the lame, the blind, and you will be blessed. Although they cannot repay you, you will be repaid at the resurrection of the righteous" (Luke 14:13–14).

This is the way Jesus loved those around Him, and it's the way He's loved us too. As Paul explains, "when we were still powerless, Christ died for the ungodly. Very rarely will anyone die for a righteous person, though for a good person someone might possibly dare to die. But God demonstrates his own love for us in this: While we were still sinners, Christ died for us" (Rom. 5:6–8).

Safe and secure in His Father's love for Him, Jesus ignores pride's seductive whisper and pursues the marginalized. He welcomes little children—those who had nothing to offer Him—and grows downright angry with His disciples when they try to send them away. He welcomes the sinners and eats with tax collectors. He reaches out to the widows and the prostitutes. He invites ordinary fishermen to become His honored students. He reveals His identity to a lonely and abandoned Samaritan woman.

Time after time, Jesus eschews the powerful and influential to seek out the lowly and downtrodden. Instead of going up to Jerusalem to seek the priests' approval or to build a coalition with the powerful, Jesus hangs out with the sinners, the tax collectors, the sick, and the weak.

He loves the "least of these" and elevates them to a place of honor again and again. He calls His disciples to likewise serve those who cannot repay and to do good to those who cannot return the favor, not for public praise, but for their heavenly Father's eyes and approval only.

CHALLENGE

As humans, we are turned inward on ourselves,[1] constantly seeking our own good, even when it looks like we're serving others. Are you ever tempted to show more love or generosity toward those who can reciprocate? This week, seek out one person who can't repay you (whether a child in your neighborhood, a widow in your congregation, or a homeless person on the street), and love them lavishly, privately, without expectation of being seen or known by anyone but Jesus.

PRAYER

Precious Jesus, You who are perfect love, forgive me for loving selfishly, doing good to those who can reward me with their praise, appreciation, and reciprocation. Thank You for loving me when I had nothing to give You. Help me love others like You love. Amen.

FOR FURTHER STUDY

Matthew 18:2–4, 10–14; 25:31–46; Mark 10:13–15;
Luke 14:13–14; John 4:4–30; 13:1; 1 John 4:19–21

JESUS OFFERS SECOND CHANCES

"Woman, where are they? Has no one condemned you?"
JOHN 8:10

READ THE STORY: JOHN 8:1-11

The Pharisees were trying to trap Jesus, completely disregarding the woman in question. She was a convenient and disposable pawn to play in their political maneuvers.

Let's put ourselves in her shoes for a moment. How did the Pharisees catch her? Most likely by stationing two or three witnesses either in the room or at the keyhole. They either heard of a possible affair or set it up deliberately to trap Jesus.

Along with the public humiliation of being dragged through the streets as an adulteress, the woman would have also faced possible betrayal from the one she had given herself to (one possible explanation for why the man is conveniently excused by the Pharisees instead of brought forward for capital punishment alongside her). She knew what she had done deserved punishment, but no one had been stoned for adultery for ages (as it wasn't permitted under Roman law without a governor's permission).[1]

There she stood, alone, condemned already, shame-faced, and silent. For what could she say to defend herself? She was as good as dead. But worse, she was stripped of her dignity and identity. Even if she escaped with her life, her reputation would be forever besmirched, her family dishonored, her future ruined. Nothing would ever be the same again.

The Pharisees continued pestering Jesus, but He remained oddly silent, scribbling in the sand. Many are fascinated by this detail of Jesus writing in the sand. What did He write? Why did He do this? We don't know. The text doesn't tell us because that's not the point of the story. Let's not get caught up in exciting speculations and miss this: Jesus' love rescues this vulnerable woman and affirms her humanity and dignity, offering her a second chance at life.

He does this by turning the Pharisees' self-righteousness on themselves. According to Mosaic law, witnesses who reported adultery would be the first to cast the stones, yet at Jesus' pronouncement—"Let any one of you who is without sin be the first to throw a stone at her"—not one dares be the first. Once confident and critical, the Pharisees recognized their sinful state before the holy and righteous God they claimed to serve and dropped their stones, the older ones leaving first.

The only one without sin worthy to cast the first stone is left alone with the woman. He finally straightens up and faces her. "Woman, where are they?" She looks around bewildered. He prods, "Has no one condemned you?"

Her eyes dart around until they finally lock on His steady gaze. "No one, sir." Note the respect in her voice. The trepidation. The incredulity.

But there was still One who could condemn her, and He was looking straight at her. Certainly, He saw her guilt. Surely, He knew her heart. Possibly, she held her breath.

"Then neither do I condemn you," Jesus declares.

Whereas the Pharisees had used their words to condemn the downtrodden, the Word made flesh called into existence an unimaginable new beginning: "Go now and leave your life of sin."

Quite simply, these men had pounced on a vulnerable woman to exploit her for their own shady purposes. Jesus saw through their facade, turned it on them, and offered this woman what she did not deserve: forgiveness, hope, and a future.

CHALLENGE

We don't know what happened next, but let's sit and reflect. Have you ever felt exploited by those in religious power? Have you ever sat in condemnation of others, whether secretly judging them or openly gossiping about them? How do Jesus' words to the Pharisees and to the woman speak to you today?

PRAYER

Lord Jesus, You alone are worthy to judge the world, and one day You will return to judge the living and the dead. Forgive me for placing myself in the judge's seat, condemning my fellow humans. Thank You for Your love, deep enough to forgive my deepest sins, great enough to cover my most shameful secrets, strong enough to call forth a bright hope and future. Oh, how great is Your love for me and for all Your children. Help me love others as You do. Amen.

FOR FURTHER STUDY

Jeremiah 29:10–14; Matthew 7:1–5; John 3:16–17;
Romans 8:1–3

JESUS SEEKS THE LOST

"The Son of Man came to seek and to save the lost."
LUKE 19:10

Jesus heard that [the Jewish leaders] had thrown him
out [of the synagogue], and when he found him, he said,
"Do you believe in the Son of Man?"
JOHN 9:35

READ THE STORY: JOHN 9:1-34

Throughout the Gospels, we read of Jesus performing miraculous signs that testified to His identity as the One sent from God to rescue His people. And while these miraculous signs served as public testimony to His identity, we also witness Jesus' intense, personal love for each person He touched.

We read in John 9 how Jesus healed a man who was blind since birth. For those of us raised in church, it's easy to gloss over the details, blobbing together all the stories of blind people seeing into one massive text. But this narrative is singular in that it's the only time Jesus heals a person who had been *born* blind, and this detail is critically important.

Other prophets and men of God had opened the eyes of the blind. But no one had ever given sight to someone born blind, as the man himself testifies before the Jewish leaders. In fact, giving sight to those born blind was one of the characteristics unique to the long-awaited Messiah. Jesus' claim to be the light of the world right before performing this miraculous healing clearly points to His ownership of the Messiah title, as the man who receives sight clearly understands. But his courage to stand against the Jewish leaders and publicly proclaim Jesus as the Messiah earns him expulsion from the community and banishment from the synagogue.

This man who had once been isolated from his community by his physical infirmity is now isolated by his social ostracism. But Jesus, hearing that he had been thrown out, seeks him and finds him.

What would compel Jesus to take time out of His busy schedule of teaching and healing the masses to seek out a single man?

His heart of love, of course.

Jesus lives out the parable of the lost sheep, leaving the crowd behind to go after this man who must have felt lost and alone in his newfound world. The Good Shepherd, upon finding His sheep, "joyfully puts it on his shoulders and goes home" (see Luke

15:3–7). So Jesus, finding this man invites him to place his destiny into His care, and believing in Jesus, the man falls to His feet in worship. He had been blind, and now he saw. He had been lost, and now he was found. He had been thrown out of his community, but now he was finally brought home.

CHALLENGE

Jesus' love compels Him to seek and to save the lost. Does that same love beat wildly in your heart as well? Or are you comfortable staying with the ninety-nine who are safe and sound? In the margins or in your journal, take time to write the names of those who are far from Jesus, and ask Him to compel you with His love to seek them that He may save them.

PRAYER

Good Shepherd, You sought me while I was lost, and You brought me home to Yourself. I want to learn to love like You love. Guard me from self-righteousness and spiritual blindness like the Pharisees. Give me eyes to see the lost and to go after them. Amen.

FOR FURTHER STUDY

Psalm 146:8; Isaiah 35:4–6; 42:6–7; 61:1–3; Luke 4:14–21; 7:18–24; John 9:35–10:21

JESUS IS NOT SELF-SEEKING

*Then he [Jesus] put his hands on her, [the crippled woman]
and immediately she straightened up and praised God. . . . [But] the
synagogue leader said to the people, "There are six days for work.
So come and be healed on those days, not on the Sabbath."*

LUKE 13:13–14

"For I desire mercy, not sacrifice."

HOSEA 6:6

READ THE STORY: LUKE 13:10-17

As humans, we like to be liked. As soon as we walk into a room, we scan the area and adjust our body language, volume, and actions to match the vibe of the room. Whether we admit it or not, we want others to like us, and we carefully measure our words and actions to secure others' admiration.

We're naturally selfish, and we're experts at playing games to come out on top. Even within our religious circles, rule-keeping often masquerades as righteousness in an attempt to manage others' perception of us and subtly ensure God's approval too.

And once again, Jesus flips our scripts and reveals the sinfulness of selfish hearts, uncovering a better way.

It's a Sabbath, and Jesus is teaching in a synagogue when His gaze scans the crowd and falls on a woman who is crippled. She's hunched, her spine painfully distorted for eighteen years. Others see her too but hardly notice her—she's a novelty for newcomers but invisible to those who see her week after week.

But not to Jesus. He refuses to ignore our infirmities. Jesus interrupts His teaching and calls her forward. Her heart beats faster as she shuffles toward the front. *Have I broken the law without realizing it? Why is He calling attention to me? Why can't He just leave me be?*

We can't know exactly what she was thinking, but we know she obeyed, and as soon as she reached Jesus, He touched her and set her free of her infirmity.

Immediately, the woman straightens up and begins praising God. The synagogue leader is furious at this perceived breaching of Sabbath law, and publicly scolds the crowds. "Come get your healing on the other six days," he says. While he doesn't openly rebuke Jesus, the leader's unspoken accusation hangs thick in the air, and Jesus doesn't hesitate to respond.

These self-righteous people were caught up in their own selfishness, manipulating the law to take care of their own wants, while ignoring the needs of others. But Jesus was not impressed with their rule-keeping, and He didn't care for their opinion of Him. He had come to seek and to save the lost, and He rebuked those who twisted God's commands to protect their own farm animals but oppress the very ones those laws were meant to protect. The whole point of the Sabbath was to celebrate God's rule over the world and to rest in His work—Jesus was bringing the full meaning of the Sabbath to bear on this woman's life, setting her free to rest on the day of rest.

In revealing their hypocrisy, Jesus humiliated His opponents and reinforced God's original intention with His laws: to love Him and to love one another. Jesus could have waited to heal this woman until after He had finished teaching. He could have put it off until the next day. He could have searched out a quiet moment to deliver her privately.

But Jesus wasn't trying to win their approval. He cared more for this suffering woman than He did for what others thought of Him. Because love looks out for the interests of others, it's not interested in how others think we look.

CHALLENGE

How often do we get so caught up in what others think of us that we ignore the hurt of those around us? The next time you walk into a room, look around not to ascertain how you measure up, but to seek and find the person who needs a friend. Then walk up to them and strike up a conversation, looking for ways to communicate Jesus' love toward them.

PRAYER

Lord Jesus, forgive me for the ways in which I selfishly ignore others in seeking my own good. Give me Your love for those my community scorns or ignores, and help me go out of my way to show them Your love. Amen.

FOR FURTHER STUDY

Exodus 20:8–11; Matthew 9:12–13; Luke 14:1–6

JESUS WEEPS

Jesus wept. Then the Jews said, "See how he loved him!"

JOHN 11:35–36

Love does not delight in evil.

1 CORINTHIANS 13:6

READ THE STORY: JOHN 11:1-44

Having heard of His friend Lazarus's illness, Jesus decided to delay His departure, even though Mary and Martha were hoping for Him to come immediately and heal their brother. The way John describes this detail suggests that it was Jesus' love for these siblings that caused Him to wait.

Jesus was confident that Lazarus's sickness would highlight God's glory, and He even tells His disciples that "Lazarus is dead, and for your sake I am glad I was not there, so that you may believe. But let us go to him." Heading back into Galilean territory meant certain death for Jesus, because the Jewish leaders were trying to stone Him, and once Jesus entered Judea, His enemies would have authority to arrest Him.

Yet knowing that He was walking toward His death, Jesus still made His way to Lazarus's house. At this point, He knew Lazarus was dead. And He also knew that He would raise him back to life and cause many to marvel and believe in Him. And yet, even knowing these things did not inoculate Jesus to the grief of losing a loved one.

Upon His arrival, Jesus is greeted by Martha and witnesses her grief-stricken heart. "If you had been here," she tells Him, "my brother would not have died," and Jesus goes on to assure her that her brother will live again. Their conversation seems heady and intellectual as they discuss the theology of the resurrection of the dead, until Jesus reveals a new facet of His identity: "I am the resurrection and the life." There it is again. I AM—a declaration of divinity that brings relief, and Martha declares her faith in Jesus.

All seems hopeful, especially as we know that Jesus is planning to resurrect Lazarus—which makes it all the more striking when, upon encountering Mary's brokenheartedness, Jesus Himself breaks down in heart-wrenching sobs. Even knowing that He would resurrect Lazarus, Jesus still mourned over his death.

Jesus, the Creator of life, grieved sin's theft of life in this family. Even though He knew He would resurrect Lazarus just moments later.

Jesus grieved the perversity of death in the world: the way it tears families apart, the way it mars His perfect creation, and the way it causes pain and sadness.

And He wept.

Love that celebrates people's joy but does not mourn their grief is not love at all—it is superficial opportunism.

Grief takes courage. It takes energy. It requires sacrifice, especially when joining others in a sorrow that is not our own. But grief is also the gateway to joy, as one day Jesus will return to dwell with His people in bodily form, vanquishing death and sickness, mourning, crying, and pain once and for all.

CHALLENGE

Jesus doesn't expect us to come to Him with a smile plastered on our faces. He welcomes us to come to Him with all our brokenness, our grief, and our heartache. And He weeps with us in our sorrow. He empathizes with us in our tears. Is there an area of your life that you haven't allowed yourself to grieve? Using Scripture like Psalm 88 as a guide, lament the brokenness in your life, and let Jesus' presence comfort you, even as He weeps with you.

PRAYER

Oh, Jesus, how my heart breaks for the wickedness of sin and death in this world and in my own life. Give me courage to confront the brokenness of my past. Allow me to grieve the wrong done to me and the wrong I've done toward others. Comfort me with Your presence in my grief. Turn Your ear to hear me, and teach me how to weep with others who weep. Amen.

FOR FURTHER STUDY

Genesis 50:20; Psalms 18; 44; 56:8; 88; Ecclesiastes 3:4;
Romans 8:19–23; 12:15–18; Revelation 21:3–5

*E*ver wonder how to keep Easter centered on Jesus? The activities below range from hands-on crafts that help you better understand Scripture to new spins on ancient disciplines like fasting, prayer, and almsgiving. They can be used by adults or adapted for children. Pick one or more activities to prepare your heart to celebrate Jesus this Easter.

* **Download gospel-centered Easter coloring pages** and listen to an audio reading of Jesus' final days, His death, burial, and resurrection as you color.

* **Give up a luxury during the remainder of Lent**, like dessert, fancy drinks, clothes shopping, or entertainment. Invite your family to join you, but please don't make this obligatory. Rather, model the joy of giving up a good gift for the purpose of discovering the better gift of Jesus' sustaining presence. (Learn more about the joy of fasting in my book *Full: Food, Jesus, and the Battle for Satisfaction*.)

* **Sponsor a child with the money you save by fasting**, and pray for them each week. Consider also writing them a letter once a month and mailing them an Easter coloring page.

✳ **Read aloud books that share deep theological truths about Easter in age-appropriate ways.** Some of our favorites include *Holy Week: An Emotions Primer* by Danielle Hitchen (for babies and toddlers); *The Jesus Storybook Bible* by Sally Lloyd-Jones (preschool through preteen); *The Garden, the Curtain, and the Cross* by Carl Laferton (school-aged children); and *The Passion of the King of Glory* by Russ Ramsey (for teenagers and young adults).

✳ **Write out a family intention of Lent** to remind yourself of the purpose of this season. Answer the question: "Why do we observe Lent?" It could be a simple answer like, "We observe Lent to become like Jesus and to walk closely with Him," or your own personalized Lenten family intention. As a visual reminder of your Lenten intention, fill a small plate with sand and stones to remember the Israelites' wanderings because of their disobedience (Josh. 5:6) and Jesus' forty-day wilderness testing and obedience (Matt. 4:1–11).

WEEK FIVE

WEEK FIVE CELEBRATION

If you're going through this devotional with your family, you can visit uncoveringthelove.com, print out the questions and Scripture readings on separate slips of paper, and distribute them among your family members in order to involve everyone. Most of these components are simple enough for even small children to read alone or with help.

OPEN WITH A SIMPLE PRAYER.

LIGHT THE LAST THREE CANDLES ON YOUR LENTEN WREATH, IF USING ONE.

READ THE FOLLOWING VERSES ALOUD:

> "When you were dead in your sins and in the uncircumcision of your flesh, God made you alive with Christ. And having disarmed the powers and authorities, he made a public spectacle of them, triumphing over them by the cross." — Colossians 2:13, 15

SOMEONE ASKS:

> Why did Jesus have to die?

SOMEONE RESPONDS:

> Jesus died to disarm the powers of sin, death, and the devil.

Snuff out another candle on your Lenten wreath, if using one.

Take turns reading through this part of the gospel story:

John 10:11–18

Discussion Questions:

1. The Good Shepherd protects His sheep with His own life. How does this demonstrate the love of Jesus?

2. Verse 18 explains that Jesus has the authority to lay down His life and pick it back up again. What does this tell us about Jesus?

3. What do you want to say in response to Jesus?

Sing the following song together:

"Victory in Jesus" by Eugene Monroe Bartlett

As you begin reading the daily devotions this week, light the last two candles and thank Jesus for the ways He demonstrates His love toward you. After you've finished your daily reading and prayer, blow out the remaining candles.

JESUS LOVES THE SELF-RIGHTEOUS

"Teacher," he declared, "all these I have kept since I was a boy."
Jesus looked at him and loved him. "One thing you lack," he said.
"Go, sell everything you have and give to the poor, and you
will have treasure in heaven. Then come, follow me."

MARK 10:20–21

READ THE STORY: MARK 10:17-22

How many parents have been embarrassed by their children's temper tantrums in the grocery store? Or their lack of manners upon receiving a gift? Anyone who has raised a child understands the importance of teaching their children to show respect, to obey the rules, and to become an upstanding citizen of society.

But any good parent knows that more important than a child's external compliance is their internal sensitivity to God's Spirit and their wholehearted surrender to Him.

Here we see Jesus' love for a young man who, by all external measures, perfectly fulfilled the law of Moses: he obeyed and honored his parents; he was honest in his business transactions; he was truthful in his testimony; he was pure in his relationships.

Any parent would be thrilled to have their child grow up and become an upstanding citizen in society as this young man had become. So, at first, Jesus' demand to sell all he had seems unfair. After all, this man was doing pretty well, wasn't he? Why place this undue burden on him, especially when He hadn't asked the same of other rich disciples, like Matthew, Zacchaeus, and Nicodemus?

Such a strict command seems uncharacteristically harsh, until we read the text carefully and realize: Jesus looked at him and loved him.

This young man seems self-assured in his rule-keeping and has no problem showering Jesus with praise. Certainly others looked up to him and respected him. But in His love, Jesus studied him carefully and looked past the externals, pushing to the deeper heart issues this young man was facing.

Externally, he seemed perfect. Internally, he was wrestling with greed and idolatry, and these sins were threatening to suffocate the life out of him—and to keep him from finding eternal life in Jesus. Moved with compassion, Jesus clearly articulates the unspoken sins that overrun this young man's heart and calls him out, not to shame him, but to invite him to a life of true fruitfulness.

Jesus' good seed cannot grow roots and bear fruit in a heart that is suffocated by the weeds of the worries of this life, the deceitfulness of wealth, and the desires for more and more stuff (see Mark 4:19). It would be callous and unloving of Jesus to allow those sins to continue growing; it is His love that compels Him to reach in and yank them out by the roots, allowing the soil of our hearts to remain receptive to His Word and to produce a crop that's a hundredfold. If only we'd let Him.

But repentance was too much of a sacrifice for this man. Jesus' intuition was spot-on, and the rich young man went away sad. Forced to choose between money and Jesus, he had chosen money. Jesus had seen him. Jesus knew him. And Jesus had lovingly called him to a richer life. But he wouldn't have it.

CHALLENGE

We can be quick to read this story and measure our own riches against the wealthiest people we know, excusing ourselves so that this teaching doesn't apply to us. But let's invite Jesus' Spirit to search us and show us what steals our affection, whether it's money, status, food, family, shopping, social media, or something else. Take a few minutes today to pray and ask God to reveal any weeds growing in your own heart. Then confess those sins of idolatry and ask Him to make your heart tender toward Him, receptive to His Word, and fruitful in the harvest of His love.

PRAYER

Precious Jesus, I confess that my heart is overrun with sin that woos me away from you. Till up the soil of my heart, Lord Jesus, and put to death any affection that competes with wholehearted adoration of You. I renounce any good or evil thing that comes between me and You. Take it all, and help me desire You alone. Amen.

FOR FURTHER STUDY

Matthew 10:37–38; Mark 4:1–20; 10:21; John 12:1–8;
1 Timothy 6:8–10; 1 John 2:15–16

JESUS IS NOT EASILY ANGERED

*The crowd rebuked [the blind men] and told them to be quiet,
but they shouted all the louder, "Lord, Son of David, have mercy
on us!" . . . Jesus had compassion on them and touched their eyes.
Immediately, they received their sight and followed him.*

MATTHEW 20:31, 34

Love . . . is not easily angered.

1 CORINTHIANS 13:5

READ THE STORY: MATTHEW 20:29-34

We all deal with minor annoyances every day, whether it's morning traffic on our commute, milk spilled on freshly washed floors, or noisy children demanding attention while we're on our phones.

People in Jesus' time were easily annoyed too.

As Jesus and His disciples were leaving Jericho accompanied by a large crowd, two blind beggars on the side of the road heard the commotion, discerned it was the famed teacher, and decided today was their lucky day.

As beggars, their presence alone would be irritating enough to some. Their unwashed bodies and tattered clothes would have caused those passing by to wrinkle their noses and avert their gazes. But rather than blend into the background, they were causing a ruckus as they tried to make themselves heard above the crowd. The men and women rebuked them; they were trying to hear Jesus.

But these desperate men wouldn't be shut up. They just kept calling louder and louder: "Lord, Son of David, have mercy on us!"

Imagine the crowd's annoyance turning into anger. Why couldn't the two men just be quiet already? Didn't they realize they're interfering with their ability to get close to Jesus?

But Jesus stops and calls the men to Himself.

Where others were angered by the men's persistence, Jesus rewarded them with His presence. What others experienced as inconvenience, Jesus experienced as compassion, welcoming interruptions as opportunities to love those He had come to save. He refused to allow others' annoyance to keep these men away. And as soon as their eyes were opened, they immediately followed Jesus. Here was a man who finally cared for them.

Anger in itself is not sinful—it can be a healthy recognition that things are not as they ought to be. But when anger is directed against someone who inconveniences us, that is not righteous anger but rather self-centered anger. Jesus is quick to extinguish anger that puts people down because it's antithetical to who Jesus is and how He loves.

Jesus was angered when God's image-bearers were trampled on and abused for others' selfish gains. Any action that pushes one's own agenda at the cost of someone else's dignity is an affront to God's loving nature and cause for righteous anger. But anger aroused from personal inconvenience reveals our own pride, selfishness, and lack of love.

Many people try to pitch an "Old Testament angry God" against a "New Testament loving Jesus," yet such caricatures completely misrepresent the unified nature of God the Father, Son, and Holy Spirit. It is precisely God's love that compels Him to anger when He calls out the wickedness of those who abuse the helpless for their own selfish gains. It is God's perfect love that pours out wrath on those who seek their own advancement at the cost of others' well-being. And it's that same perfect love in Jesus that causes Him to lash out at the religious leaders of His time who abused those placed in their spiritual care and those who made money off of worshipers in the temple.

That same perfect love compels Jesus to show compassion toward these two blind men who inconvenienced the crowds and incurred their wrath. Jesus' compassion and His anger both flow from the same heart of love—love not of self, but love of God and love for others.

Throughout the Old Testament, God's anger is kindled by those who abuse the poor and helpless for their own selfish gains, and we witness this same anger in Jesus (see Mark 7:5–13).

It is Jesus' love that compels Him to anger against those who abuse and misuse the helpless. His anger burned against the disciples when they tried to keep the little children from Him. His anger burned against the moneychangers who made a profit off of those who came to worship at the temple. His anger burned against the religious leaders who misled the people placed in their spiritual charge. The God of both the Old Testament and the New Testament is the same God, made fully known in Jesus Christ, whose anger burns out of love.

CHALLENGE

Think back on the last time you were angry. Was it caused by witnessing injustice done against others or a perceived inconvenience against yourself? What does your anger reveal about your own heart? If Jesus were sitting across from you, would He join you in rebuking those you are angry with, or would He turn and rebuke you? Sit for a moment with these questions, and ask the Spirit to reveal any sinful anger in your life you need to confess and to fill you with His love instead.

PRAYER

Dear Jesus, I acknowledge that I don't love perfectly. I can be easily angered, but usually because I'm not happy with how I'm treated. Forgive me for my selfishness. Remove this anger from my heart and replace it with Your love. Break my heart for what breaks Yours. Let it be Your love that compels me to righteous anger toward those who abuse others, and let it be Your love that compels me to forgive those who hurt me. In my anger, keep me from sinning against You and others. Teach me to love well. In Jesus' name. Amen.

FOR FURTHER STUDY

Isaiah 58; Matthew 12:11–16; 25:31–46; Mark 10:46–52;
12:38–40; Luke 9:51–56; 18:35–43; Ephesians 4:26

JESUS BELIEVES ALL THINGS

"Zacchaeus, come down immediately.
I must stay at your house today."

LUKE 19:5

Love . . . believes all things.

1 CORINTHIANS 13:7 ESV

READ THE STORY: LUKE 19:1-10

Jesus was constantly challenging the Pharisees' assumptions of right and wrong, clean and unclean, and those who are "in" and those who are "out" of God's kingdom. In their societal structure, tax collectors were at the very bottom, considered traitors because they gathered taxes on behalf of the Gentiles who ruled over them and often profited by exerting additional fines and fees to line their own pockets.

In their view, tax collectors were no better than unclean Gentiles, even though they were technically Jewish and included in God's covenant with Abraham. Those devoted to the extra traditions added to Levitical law avoided contact with tax collectors at all costs.

But Jesus sees what is hidden from others' view.

At the beginning of His public ministry, Jesus welcomed a tax collector, Matthew, to join Him as one of His disciples. Scripture tells us that when Jesus had dinner at Matthew's house that night "many tax collectors and sinners came and ate with him and his disciples" (Matt. 9:10), while the Pharisees rebuked Jesus' disciples for this suspicious association.

Now, toward the end of His public ministry, Jesus again reaches out to a tax collector, this time the notorious Zacchaeus.[2] Because of Jericho's strategic location on the border between Judea and Perea, the city would have seen significant customs duties, and Zacchaeus and his tax crew would have been considerably rich. And considerably hated.

But Jesus does not write off Zacchaeus because of his occupation. Instead, He looks at his heart. This man longs to see Jesus, risking additional ridicule by climbing into a tree to see Him over the crowds. Jesus searches him out and honors him with His presence.[3]

Zacchaeus's response reveals the true nature of his heart: he gladly hosts Jesus and His disciples, he voluntarily offers half of his possessions to the poor, and he fulfills the law by vowing to make restitution for any of his cheating.

All that, simply because Jesus invited Himself over to his house. Because in loving Zacchaeus, Jesus believes "in the best outcome for the one who has done the wrong—that wrong will be confessed and forgiven and the loved one restored to righteousness."[4] And Zacchaeus responded to Jesus' love with flourishing repentance.

In contrast, the enemy of our souls is quick to accuse us before God and to condemn us for our sins. He's the one who sows despair and hopelessness in our hearts, convincing us that we will never be rid of the sin that entangles us.

Jesus knows the state of every person's heart, and He takes time with those whose hearts are receptive to God's Word and eager to repent. He knew the state of Zacchaeus's heart, even though the Pharisees had no idea, and He acts on that belief even when no one else sees it or knows it or even believes it. Jesus believes the best, because He knows the truth about Zacchaeus that was hidden from everyone else.

It's telling that Jesus demonstrates this believing love not only toward the outcasts, like tax collectors, but also toward the religious elite, like Nicodemus. This Pharisee, a member of the Jewish ruling council, came to Jesus at night, and Jesus greeted him not with suspicion but with sincerity, welcoming his earnest questions.

Zacchaeus and Nicodemus represent two extremes on the religious spectrum, but Jesus recognized the truth of their hearts, even when they themselves failed to see it. His love watered those seeds, and they couldn't help but respond with an outpouring of love in action—Zacchaeus immediately and Nicodemus gradually.

CHALLENGE

Scripture assures us that God will complete the good work He has started in us, but sometimes His hand is hidden from our view. Think of a person in your church you're naturally suspicious of and practice believing the best about them. Thank God for being at work in their lives, and when you next see them, make a point of commending something good you've seen them do. You may just be surprised by how they respond.

PRAYER

Precious Jesus, thank You for never giving up on me. Even when I despair, You continue to believe because You Yourself are faithful. You've promised to complete the good work You've started within me, and You never break Your promises. Oh, how great is Your love for me! Help me to love those hard-to-love people in my own life and to believe in Your work within them. Amen.

FOR FURTHER STUDY

Matthew 9:9–13; John 3:1–21; 19:39–42; Ephesians 2:8–10; Philippians 1:6; Hebrews 10:19–25

JESUS IS NOT PROUD

"The Son of Man did not come to be served, but to serve."

MATTHEW 20:28

*"Now that I, your Lord and Teacher, have washed your feet,
you also should wash one another's feet."*

JOHN 13:14

READ THE STORY: JOHN 13:1–17

There's always that one job around the house that nobody wants to do. For some, it's scrubbing toilets. For others, it's emptying the dishwasher.

In first-century Palestine, it was washing feet.

Nobody wanted to wash feet.

Imagine the stench of sweat, dust, and dung; picture the callouses and ingrown toenails; feel the humility of doing what no one else wanted to do.

In fact, this job was considered so demeaning that it was reserved for the lowest of servants in a household. On this holy Passover night, Jesus and His disciples had already begun eating with their feet unwashed. No one wanted to do that job.

So in the middle of their meal, Jesus gets up, takes off His outer robe, and dons a towel. Every eye is watching His every move. Surely not! This cannot be happening. Out of everyone in the room, Jesus should have been the last person to wash anyone's feet.

For those of us who have grown up hearing this story again and again, the wrongness of the situation may have become lost on us. It's Peter's visceral reaction that helps establish the absurdity of the moment: "No, you shall never wash my feet," he tells Jesus.

Never.

This is wrong.

Maybe John should be washing feet since he's the youngest. Or perhaps Philip or Andrew should run to fetch the servant girl. But not You.

It's understandable why the disciples hesitated to volunteer for this task; even though disciples were expected to serve their rabbis, washing their teachers' feet was one service specifically not expected even of them. Let alone washing their peers' feet!

But Jesus demonstrated that in His kingdom, no person is too high for the lowest of tasks, for He Himself took on the nature of a servant though He was in very nature God. And He served not only His best friends, but the one who would betray Him, the one who would deny Him, and the ones who would desert Him.

His greatest act of love was yet to come, but washing the disciples' feet was a shocking expression of love that foretold just how low Jesus was willing to bow in order to love His own until the very end.

CHALLENGE

After Jesus sits back down to continue the Passover meal, He asks His disciples if they understand what He has done. Do you? How is He calling you to wash another's feet today? Do so, not out of obligation or consternation, but out of humble love.

PRAYER

King Jesus, You who humbled Yourself to the lowest of servant tasks, You are exalted to the highest place in heaven. I'll admit: Your example humbles me. It's hard for me to follow Your lead, but I want to. Help me lay aside my pride and any concern for my image, and empower me to kneel before others in humble service, out of love. Amen.

FOR FURTHER STUDY

Mark 10:45; John 13:1–17; Philippians 2:6–7

JESUS IS PATIENT

Jesus said to him, "Have I been with you so long,
and you still do not know me, Philip? Whoever has seen me
has seen the Father. How can you say, 'Show us the Father'?"

JOHN 14:9 ESV

Love is patient.

1 CORINTHIANS 13:4

READ THE STORY: JOHN 14

Have you ever wished you could have walked with Jesus? Been one of His disciples?

What a privilege to live with Jesus for three years, spending day and night with the Teacher, watching Him not just when He commanded the attention of thousands, but watching Him slumber in the helm of a boat tossed by waves. Watching Him play with little children. Watching Him enjoy a well-roasted leg of lamb. Watching Him command the winds to quiet and the dead to rise.

If anyone had a front-row seat to witness Jesus' divinity, it was these disciples.

Yet even these twelve men didn't quite comprehend Jesus.

After all they had seen, they still didn't understand who Jesus was. After the Last Supper, Jesus comforts His disciples, but Peter, Thomas, and Judas (not Judas Iscariot) all ask questions for clarification. Philip speaks up, saying, "Lord, show us the Father, and that will be enough for us." In these last moments with Jesus, he wanted a theophany—a visible display of God Himself.

After all He had done, Jesus could have been understandably disappointed with Philip's request.

Consider how patient Jesus had been with His disciples. He interpreted parables for them. He gave them unique glimpses into His power over stormy winds and waves. He gently rebuked their lack of faith while simultaneously reinforcing their faith. He redirected their attention when they bickered among themselves about who was the greatest. He corrected them when they wanted to call down fire from heaven on the inhospitable. Every step of their three-year journey, Jesus had been infinitely patient with them, answering their questions and reorienting their sight to see God's kingdom, not as they expected it, but as Jesus was bringing it.

And here they are, on their very last night together, and still they don't get it.

"Have I been with you so long, and you still do not know me, Philip?" He asks.

But rather than grow exasperated with Philip and His other disciples, notice Jesus' patience with them. He doesn't grow angry or insult their intelligence (though such a rebuke might be warranted). He reminds Philip that he had seen God this whole time he had been with Jesus, because: "No one has ever seen God, but the one and only Son, who is himself God and is in closest relationship with the Father, has made him known" (John 1:18).

Throughout His three-year tenure with His disciples, Jesus revealed His Father through His character, His words, and His miracles. He lived and loved before them, and His greatest demonstration of love was yet to come.

CHALLENGE

Who do you struggle to show patience toward? Perhaps a child who questions your parenting or a coworker who tests your limits? Ask Jesus to work His patience in you and through you as you love those people. The next time you're tempted to respond sternly, consider giving yourself a time-out, stepping away from the situation for a few minutes to take a few breaths and ask God to show you how you can reveal His character. Then go out and love that person as Jesus loved His disciples.

PRAYER

Precious Jesus, Your patience knows no limits. Thank You for the patience You demonstrated toward Your disciples, because I can so relate to their limitations. Thank You for being patient with me on my imperfect journey of walking with You. Help me also patiently love my family and friends. Amen.

FOR FURTHER STUDY

Mark 4:35–41; Luke 9:51–55; John 1:16–18;
1 Corinthians 13:4; Galatians 5:22–24

*E*ver wonder how to keep Easter centered on Jesus? The activities below range from hands-on crafts that help you better understand Scripture to new spins on ancient disciplines like fasting, prayer, and almsgiving. They can be used by adults or adapted for children. Pick one or more activities to prepare your heart to celebrate Jesus this Easter.

✻ **Craft paper crowns from construction paper** to represent the crowns of righteousness Jesus gives us in exchange for our sins (see Isa. 61:1–3). Write the word "righteous" in bold lettering and decorate with stickers and jewels. Wear your crown to remember what Jesus accomplished on the cross.

✻ **Bake homemade (or store-bought) soft pretzels**. Tradition has it that pretzels were invented by a sixth-century Italian monk who twisted scraps of dough to resemble arms crossed over the chest in prayer. While the pretzels rest, read Luke 22:39–46 and John 17 and discuss Jesus' time of prayer in the garden of Gethsemane. While they bake, spend some time in prayer.

✻ **Drink no beverages but water for the remainder of Lent**, and donate the money you save on coffee or other drinks to an organization that provides clean water to impoverished communities.

❉ **Mail homemade Easter greeting cards** to grandparents, aunts, uncles, and other family members to spread the joy of Jesus' resurrection hope. Pray for them specifically this week.

❉ **Buy or make your own resurrection eggs** to creatively retell the story of Easter. Each plastic egg contains an item that corresponds to a moment of Holy Week (e.g., a small leaf for Palm Sunday, a dime for Judas's betrayal, a saltine cracker for the Last Supper, a piece of cloth for foot washing, etc.). Find links to purchase or make your own at uncoveringthelove.com.

BONUS CONTENT

Go to uncoveringthelove.com to find step-by-step tutorials, download a free printable activity sheet, and discover other helpful resources to observe Lent together as a family.

WEEK SIX

*I*f you're going through this devotional with your family, you can visit *uncoveringthelove.com*, print out the questions and Scripture readings on separate slips of paper, and distribute them among your family members in order to involve everyone. Most of these components are simple enough for even small children to read alone or with help.

OPEN WITH A SIMPLE PRAYER.

LIGHT THE LAST TWO CANDLES ON YOUR LENTEN WREATH, IF USING ONE.

READ THE FOLLOWING VERSE ALOUD:

> "For Christ also suffered once for sins, the righteous for the unrighteous, to bring you to God. He was put to death in the body but made alive in the Spirit."
> — 1 Peter 3:18

SOMEONE ASKS:

> Why did Jesus have to die?

SOMEONE RESPONDS:

> Jesus died to bring us into a right relationship with God.

SNUFF OUT ANOTHER CANDLE ON YOUR LENTEN WREATH, IF USING ONE.

John 14:1–10

1. Jesus explains to Philip that He is the way to the Father. What does this tell us about God?

2. What questions do you have about today's passage?

3. What do you want to say in response to Jesus?

"Man of Sorrows" by Philip B. Bliss (1838)

As you begin reading the daily devotions this week, light the last candle and thank Jesus for the ways He demonstrates His love toward you. After you've finished your daily reading and prayer, blow out the remaining candles.

JESUS LOVES THE UNLOVABLE

"If you love those who love you, what credit is that to you?
Even sinners love those who love them."

LUKE 6:32

He [Judas] approached Jesus to kiss him, but Jesus asked him,
"Judas, are you betraying the Son of Man with a kiss?"

LUKE 22:47–48

READ THE STORY: JOHN 13:1-30

Because God loves justice, He must hate wickedness. But how does this square with the love of Jesus?

The writer of Proverbs lists seven things that God hates, and Judas Iscariot embodies as least four of them (see Prov. 6:16–19).

We don't know many details about Judas, but as part of the

Twelve, he had made a commitment to follow Jesus; he had received power and authority to preach and perform miracles; he had walked with Jesus, watched His miracles, and listened to His teachings. To onlookers, Judas was one of the chosen.

And indeed he was. Because Jesus chose to love Judas.

Even though Jesus knew from the beginning that Judas would betray Him, He still invited Judas to be with Him and be part of His ministry. Jesus gave him the same opportunities as the others to choose life and obedience. Jesus protected Judas and kept him safe from harm, up to the moment Judas rejected and betrayed Him.

In John 12:1–8, we see a dark foreshadowing when Judas criticizes Mary's expensive anointing of Jesus the week before His death. He scoffs at such an outlandish offering: the little flask of perfume would have cost a year's salary—the equivalent of $25,000 in our day.[1] In Judas's estimation, Jesus is not worth such a costly display of affection. In fact, Judas sells Jesus for a fraction of the cost, just four month's wages—the redemption price for a slave.[2]

Judas didn't treasure Jesus. And yet, Jesus loved him.

On the last night, in the most intimate setting around the Passover meal, Jesus loved Judas to the very end. Washing the feet of His betrayer was beyond human love. It could only be divine. But it came at great cost.

Jesus was not unaffected by Judas's intentions: "Jesus was troubled in spirit and testified, 'Very truly I tell you, one of you is going to betray me'" (John 13:21). He declared beforehand the tragedy that would follow to reassure His disciples that He was still in control. But He was troubled.

"Who is it?" The disciples wanted to know. They were deeply troubled. Surely none of the men in their tight band of disciples would be capable of such a heinous crime.

Dipping the paschal bread, Jesus offered it to Judas, who was likely seated next to Him in a place of honor.[3] Feeding another person bread was both an intimate act of friendship and an open display of honor. As Jesus was holding out the piece of bread, certainly Judas felt His penetrating gaze offering him one last chance to turn from his wicked plans and cling to Jesus for forgiveness and life. He had just heard Jesus' words. He still had a choice to repent.

Yet he took hold of the bread, and in that moment, Satan entered into him.

How Jesus' heart must have broken at Judas's choice!

Yet He did not rebuke him, nor lash out in anger, nor seek revenge, but simply told him to leave: "What you are about to do, do quickly." They both knew what He was talking about, though none of the others understood. And in this intimate exchange, Jesus spared Judas public humiliation, showing incredible love.

Even when Judas walked up to Jesus to betray Him with the

most intimate expression of love—a kiss—Jesus called him His friend. It's a heart-wrenching scene. "Judas," Jesus prods, "are you betraying the Son of Man with a kiss?" (Luke 22:48). Hear Jesus' sorrow in His words. Hear His love shattered by rejection.

Would Jesus have forgiven Judas even at this point? Without a doubt. Look no further than Saul's conversion to see that no sin is too hideous for Jesus to pardon for those who come to Him. Jesus' perfect love extends to the unlovable, but will never force acceptance. Love that does not allow rejection is no love at all—it is dictatorial adulation. And that is not our Jesus. Though He deserves the worship of all and commands the praise of angels, He invites us to respond in love of our own free will.

CHALLENGE

Have you ever loved someone who did not love you back? How did that affect your love for them? Have you ever been rejected or betrayed by someone you thought loved you? How has this affected your view of Jesus' love for you?

PRAYER

Lord Jesus, Oh, how great is Your love! That while I was unlovable, Your love sought me still. Thank You that You love me not because of my devotion to You, but apart from my response to You. Help me love those hard to love in my life with the love You Yourself have shown me. Amen.

FOR FURTHER STUDY

Exodus 21:32; Psalms 41:9; 89:14; Proverbs 6:16–19;
Matthew 26:48–50; Luke 22:1–7; 17:12–19; Romans 5:10

JESUS DOESN'T GIVE UP

He went away a second time and prayed, "My Father,
if it is not possible for this cup to be taken away unless I drink it,
may your will be done." When he came back, he again found them
sleeping, because their eyes were heavy. So he left them and went
away once more and prayed the third time, saying the same thing.

MATTHEW 26:42–44

Love . . . always perseveres.

1 CORINTHIANS 13:7

READ THE STORY: MATTHEW 26:36–46

On the hardest night of His life, Jesus had a panic attack.

Earlier, Jesus had given the Passover meal a new meaning: it would be a remembrance of God's miraculous deliverance— not only from the Egyptians, but also from the enemy of their souls—and it would be a herald of Jesus' kingdom to come.

And though He knew the victory that awaited Him in the end,

Jesus didn't speed into His arrest and crucifixion like a superhero with a cape.

No. He wrestled against it. By God's bountiful grace, He preserved for us in the Gospels this heartbreaking scene where Jesus agonizes in the garden of Gethsemane, pleading with His Father to find another way. "If it is possible," He sobs, "may this cup be taken from me." Jesus knew full well the battle that was about to ensue. After all, He had predicted His betrayal, His rejection, and His death.

But that didn't make it easy.

In His humanity, Jesus experienced the full spectrum of human emotions. Fear. Anxiety. Panic. Dread.

Let us be careful not to sketch a caricature of Jesus that makes Him aloft from His emotions. Because a big part of the sufferings He bore include not just the physical wounds, which were horrific, but also the emotional and social and spiritual wounds, which were dreadful.

So on this night, Jesus withdrew to His safe place and fell on His face before His Father. "And being in anguish, he prayed more earnestly, and his sweat was like drops of blood falling to the ground" (Luke 22:44). Heavy with grief, weighed down with the horror of what He knew must take place, He pleaded for an alternative. Not once, but three times.

And each time, discerning in His spirit that this was the only way forward, Jesus humbly accepted the cup of God's wrath and committed to drink it to the dregs: "May your will be done." As with His wilderness temptation, Jesus faced His own human frailty, and three times He revealed the mettle of His character, the truthfulness of His devotion to the Father, by choosing obedience over comfort.

His disciples, by contrast, couldn't even stay awake. Their friend and master was enduring the darkest night of His life, and they were dozing after some good food and good wine. Yet Jesus, rather than lash out in fury and disappointment, spends His last moments as a free man praying not just for Himself, but for His fickle friends and, amazingly, for those of us who would come to believe in Him through the ages.

When Jesus would have had every right to think or pray only for Himself, Jesus pours out His emotional and spiritual energy, wrestling in prayer for those He loves, even as those very men were sleeping a few yards away and would soon abandon Him.

CHALLENGE

Think of a time you were depending on someone you love to pull through for you, but they failed. Did that make you more likely or less likely to express love to them? In what ways does Jesus' prayer for His disciples demonstrate unconditional and selfless love? How does Jesus express this love toward you today? What would it look like for you to persevere in selfless love toward someone close to you today? Take time to pray for someone who has hurt you or abandoned you.

PRAYER

Beloved Jesus, Your love far surpasses my understanding. Thank You for never giving up on me, even when I fail You time and time again. Forgive me for becoming so easily discouraged in my love for others. Help me to persevere, to continue to love with Your perfect, unending, never-giving-up love. Amen.

FOR FURTHER STUDY

Psalm 88; Isaiah 53:3, 10; Mark 14:32–42; John 12:27; 17; 18:11

JESUS PROTECTS HIS OWN

Love . . . always protects.

1 CORINTHIANS 13:7

"If you are looking for me, then let these men go."

JOHN 18:8

READ THE STORY: JOHN 18:1-13

Having wrestled with the necessity of His atoning death, Jesus willingly submits to the Father's will. "Your will be done," He resolves.

After Jesus finishes praying, He goes out to meet the soldiers who had come to arrest Him. Notice that they did not have to track Him down, drag Him out of hiding, and beat Him into submission. "No one takes [my life] from me, but I lay it down of my own accord," He explains to His disciples. "I have authority to lay it down and authority to take it up again" (John 10:18). And then He lovingly leverages His authority to protect His disciples. Because love always protects.

Walking up to the soldiers, Jesus shields His disciples by exposing Himself, initiating the conversation: "Who is it you want?" He asks not because He doesn't know, but because He intends to take full responsibility—a physical manifestation of the spiritual reality that would follow in Jesus' substitutionary sacrifice on the cross.

"Jesus of Nazareth," they reply.

"I am he," Jesus says, and at His words the crowd draws back and falls to the ground. We have no way of knowing what caused such a response, but ironically they display more fear than the One they came to arrest. Jesus steps forward with courage and majesty, taking command of the situation. For the affirmation "I am he" doesn't just speak to His identity—it reveals His divinity. I AM, God's own name, in Jesus' mouth is terrifying to the enemy yet comforting to His own.

Though Jesus identifies Himself, the guards make no move to arrest Him. So He asks them again who they want, and again they repeat His name. Jesus affirms that He's the person they're looking for. But are they afraid? Having experienced His earth-shattering affirmation of divinity, are they terrified to lay hands on Him?

With the command of a conqueror, Jesus dictates His terms: "If you are looking for me, then let these men go." John clarifies that Jesus said this to fulfill His promise that none of those entrusted to Him would be lost (see John 17:12).

It was not unusual for authorities to arrest all accomplices when capturing the leader of a movement. Jesus' disciples risked being arrested, beaten, and punished. But Jesus had been entrusted with the lives of these men, and He had every intention of protecting them, even at great cost to Himself. He willingly absorbs all the guards' attention and negotiates the disciples' release so they may escape unharmed.

It's such a small detail in the grander story of Jesus' last hours, yet such an act of love! Even after His disciples had disappointed Him, falling asleep when Jesus had asked them to stay awake and pray with Him, even when He knew that everyone would desert Him and Peter would deny Him, still Jesus exchanged His life for His followers' freedom, like a Good Shepherd laying down His life for His sheep.

Peter, ever the impulsive one, pulls out a sword and strikes out, perhaps in an attempt to protect Jesus, not understanding that Jesus was, in fact, protecting him. Jesus sternly rebukes him, willingly walking into His arrest. No one took Him by force; He gave Himself up freely.

CHALLENGE

Who has God entrusted into your care? What threats do they face, and what would it look like to protect them today? Could you interpose yourself between your loved one and the hostile situation? Or are you to pray for God's divine protection beyond where your arms can reach?

PRAYER

Good Shepherd, even in Your arrest You cared for Your own, and to this day You stand between me and my adversary. I'm so grateful that when the accuser comes to fling his worst against me, You stand before me and protect me. There is no situation, no matter how difficult or frightening, that can assault me without Your permission; nothing that can separate me from Your love. Thank You for being my fortress and my protector. Help me rest in You. Amen.

FOR FURTHER STUDY

Isaiah 52:13–53:12; John 6:39; 10:18; 17:12

JESUS LOVES HIS ENEMIES

"Love your enemies, do good to those who hate you,
bless those who curse you, pray for those who mistreat you."

LUKE 6:27–28

One of them struck the servant of the high priest,
cutting off his right ear. But Jesus answered, "No more of this!"
And he touched the man's ear and healed him.

LUKE 22:50–51

READ THE STORY: LUKE 22:47-53

Here is the beginning of the end. Judas walks up and kisses Jesus, betraying Him with a gesture reserved for friendly greetings. The soldiers grab hold of Him. And His disciples, in a panic, whip out their two swords ready to defend their teacher.

Not waiting to be prompted, Peter slashes the ear of the high priest's servant. Did he intend to go for the neck? He was, after all a fisherman, unskilled with a sword.

In all likelihood, mayhem ensued. The temple guards were armed and a bloodbath could have easily followed. But in the midst of a chaotic situation with lots of people, Jesus focuses on one person who desperately needs help. One person who was probably bleeding profusely. One person—who was the enemy. Or so it seemed.

In this moment, Jesus exemplifies what it looks like to love your enemy and do good to him who hurts you. This last recorded healing demonstrates the extent of Jesus' love. Sometimes we can see Jesus' death on the cross for all mankind and somehow gloss over the personal nature of His sacrifice. But in this encounter, we see the personal love of Jesus for His enemies. As He was being arrested, Jesus sought to bring healing and wholeness and restoration even to those who were seeking to kill Him.

This is love. He is not self-seeking, even when we would think He had every right to be.

After all, it's fairly easy to love our friends. Even Jesus said so:

If you love those who love you, what credit is that to you? Even sinners love those who love them. And if you do good to those who are good to you, what credit is that to you? Even sinners do that. . . . But love your enemies, do good to them. . . . Then your reward will be great, and you will be children of the Most High, because he is kind to the ungrateful and wicked. Be merciful, just as your Father is merciful. (Luke 6:32–36)

This is the way of Jesus. This is the kind of love Jesus describes in the parable of the good Samaritan, who put his own plans on hold to care for the wounded Israelite, even though they were enemies (see Luke 10:25–37).

This is the kind of love Jesus' followers have demonstrated throughout history: praying for their persecutors, serving their tormentors, and forgiving their executioners. Some stories of courageous love have been preserved and passed down through the ages, while other acts of love are known only by our heavenly Father. Yet one generation after another has followed Jesus' example of sacrificial love toward those who hurt them.

And now it's our generation's turn.

CHALLENGE

As you reflect on Jesus' love for His enemies, who is "the enemy" in your life? What would it look like for you to love and do good to them this week? Go and do it.

PRAYER

Precious Jesus, even while I was Your enemy, You reconciled me to Yourself through Your death. Thank You for Your perfect love, for Your perfect forgiveness, for Your perfect life that brings me life. Help me love my enemies as You have loved me. Amen.

FOR FURTHER STUDY

Matthew 18:21–35; 26:47–56; Mark 14:43–50;
Luke 6:27–36; 22:47–53; John 18:10–11; Romans 5:6–11;
1 Corinthians 10:24, 32–33; 13:5

JESUS KEEPS NO RECORD OF WRONGS

Love . . . keeps no record of wrongs.

1 CORINTHIANS 13:5

*"Simon, Simon, Satan has asked to sift all of you as wheat.
But I have prayed for you, Simon, that your faith may not fail.
And when you have turned back, strengthen your brothers."*

LUKE 22:31

READ THE STORY: LUKE 22:54–62

What would happen if we knew people's offenses against us before they happened? How would we treat the coworker who would steal our brilliant idea next week and present it as his own? How would we view the church member who would gossip about us next month at the prayer meeting?

Even without future-telling abilities, most of us have a list of offenses once committed against us that we keep lugging around—not only reciting them mentally, but bringing them up in conversations long after the initial offense. But Scripture tells us that love keeps no record of wrongs, and Jesus beautifully models this principle in His relationship with Peter.

Peter, the oldest and boldest of the disciples, is the one we can count on to say what we're all thinking, and often got himself in trouble by acting before thinking. But no doubt about it—he was genuinely committed to Jesus. So much so, that when Jesus tells His disciples that He's going away and they can't follow, Peter responds, "Lord, why can't I follow you now? I will lay down my life for you" (John 13:37).

What was intended to be a declaration of loyalty and love had the opposite effect on Jesus. He who knew Peter's innermost thoughts and who also foresaw his every action certainly discerned Peter's sincerity. But still, Jesus was pierced to the heart. "Will you really lay down your life for me?" Hear Jesus' hurt in these words. *Really, Peter? Will you?* "Very truly I tell you, before the rooster crows, you will disown me three times!"

Crushing. There's no other way to put it.

Jesus' words to Peter would have crushed him, but the reality of Peter's denial would have crushed Jesus too. And yet the next words out of Jesus' mouth are intended to comfort His disciples: "Do not let your hearts be troubled" (John 14:1). Because Peter would have been very troubled indeed.

In John's account, Peter does not say another word until chapter 18, verse 17, when he denies being a disciple of Jesus.

Yet even with the foreknowledge of Peter's imminent denial, Jesus washed his feet, reassured him of his union with Himself (John 13:10), and invited him to join Him in a prayer vigil. He even prayed specifically for Peter, that his faith would not fail (Luke 22:31–32), and at the very moment of the third denial, Jesus turned to look straight at Peter (Luke 22:61).

What had Jesus communicated in that look? Certainly not judgment or condemnation, but love. Soul-piercing, undeserved, relentless love. Because Jesus did not hold Peter's abandonment against him. He kept no record of Peter's wrongs; He loved him to the very end.

But what's more, after His resurrection, Jesus offers Peter a valuable gift. Three times He asks Peter "do you love me?" not because Jesus needed to be reassured of Peter's love, but perhaps because Peter desperately needed the opportunity to reaffirm his love for Jesus—three times, once for each denial (see John 21).

Oh, what love! Not only does Jesus refuse to blame and shame Peter, He graciously orchestrates a conversation that would allow Peter to voice the love in his heart, a love that would burn bright to Peter's own death on a cross, in ardent devotion to his beloved Jesus.

CHALLENGE

Is there someone in your life you need to forgive and extend the invitation of reconciliation? What would loving them like Jesus look like? What can you do to move toward forgiveness?

PRAYER

Precious Jesus, You who know all things and see all things, You know the betrayals of my own heart, how I have turned from You and denied You in my affections. Forgive me. I want to love You wholeheartedly, and, in loving You, to love others too. Amen.

FOR FURTHER STUDY

Job 14:16–17; Proverbs 10:12; 17:9; Matthew 26:34, 58; Mark 14:66–72; Luke 9:28–36; 22:56–62; John 18:15–18, 25–27; 21:15–22; Acts 2:38–39; 1 Corinthians 13:5

*E*ver wonder how to keep Easter centered on Jesus? The activities below range from hands-on crafts that help you better understand Scripture to new spins on ancient disciplines like fasting, prayer, and almsgiving. They can be used by adults or adapted for children. Pick one or more activities to prepare your heart to celebrate Jesus this Easter.

❋ **Bake morning glory muffins and deliver them to neighbors** with handmade tags that say "Joy comes in the morning" (Ps. 30:5 ESV). Find the recipe in my book *Bible and Breakfast: 31 Mornings with Jesus*, or use your own family favorite recipe.

❋ **Make clay tablets to represent the Ten Commandments.** Roll out playdough and cut shapes to resemble two tablets. Carve Roman numerals I–V on the first tablet and VI–X on the second, and leave out to dry. Read Deuteronomy 5:1–22 and discuss how the commandments show we are sinners deserving punishment, but Jesus perfectly fulfilled the Law, took our punishment on the cross, and gave us His righteousness instead to bring us in a right relationship with God.

✳ **Spritz your favorite perfume or rub essential oil on each other's feet** and read Mark 14:3–9, discussing Mary's costly display of love toward Jesus. Discuss what is a costly way you may show your love for Jesus this week.

✳ **Host a night of praise and worship,** inviting friends, family, and neighbors to join you. Make enough copies of well-known song lyrics (like the ones included in the weekly celebrations) and invite your guests to bring musical instruments. Or, if you want to keep things simple, create a playlist and stream songs through a speaker. Consider setting aside time for prayer, as well as a time of communion.

✳ **Craft a hosanna banner** by writing the word on a white handkerchief and tying it to a simple branch from your backyard. Read the account of Jesus' triumphal entry into Jerusalem in John 12:12–13 and discuss how the word hosanna is a joyful cry of hope meaning "save us!" Hang your banner in a prominent place, or place it in a vase with plenty of greenery and allow it to prompt you to praise Jesus for being our Savior.

Go to uncoveringthelove.com to find step-by-step tutorials, download a free printable activity sheet, and discover other helpful resources to observe Lent together as a family.

175

WEEK SEVEN

WEEK SEVEN CELEBRATION

*I*f you're going through this devotional with your family, you can visit uncoveringthelove.com, print out the questions and Scripture readings on separate slips of paper, and distribute them among your family members in order to involve everyone. Most of these components are simple enough for even small children to read alone or with help.

OPEN WITH A SIMPLE PRAYER.

LIGHT ONLY ONE CANDLE ON YOUR LENTEN WREATH, IF USING ONE.

READ THE FOLLOWING VERSES ALOUD:

> "At present, we do not yet see everything in subjection to him. But we see him who for a little while was made lower than the angels, namely Jesus, crowned with glory and honor because of the suffering of death."
> — Hebrews 2:8–9 ESV

SOMEONE ASKS:

> Why did Jesus have to die?

SOMEONE RESPONDS:

> Jesus died to establish the kingdom of God on earth.

SNUFF OUT THE LAST CANDLE ON YOUR LENTEN WREATH, IF USING ONE.

John 18:33–19:30

Discussion Questions:

1. As we read through this account of Jesus' trial and crucifixion, what details of His kingship did you notice?

2. For those who were watching Jesus' crucifixion, it looked like His kingdom was coming to an end in His death. But what does Jesus say to Pilate about His kingdom in John 18:36–37?

3. What do you want to say in response to Jesus?

Sing the following song together:

"All Hail the Power of Jesus' Name" by Edward Perronet (1780)

As you read the daily devotions this week, ponder the snuffed candles and thank Jesus for the ways He demonstrates His love toward you.

JESUS REJOICES IN TRUTH

"You are a king, then!" said Pilate. Jesus answered,
"You say that I am a king. In fact, the reason I was born
and came into the world is to testify to the truth. Everyone on
the side of truth listens to me." "What is truth?" retorted Pilate.

JOHN 18:37–38a

Speaking the truth in love, we will grow to become in every respect
the mature body of him who is the head, that is, Christ.

EPHESIANS 4:15

READ THE STORY: JOHN 18:28-19:16

Hours before His death, Jesus engages in a lengthy conversation with an unlikely man: His executioner, Pontius Pilate. For those of us who have grown up with the Easter story, it's tempting to lump all the events of Jesus' trial into one big narrative.

But this particular exchange deserves our attention in the context of how Jesus loved people. So let's look a little closer.

On that last morning, Jesus stood before three judges: Caiaphas the high priest, King Herod Antipas, and Pontius Pilate.

It had been Caiaphas's idea to kill Jesus, so He stood before him first. The chief priests and the whole Sanhedrin were looking for false evidence to use against Jesus, but none of the false witnesses were able to build a case against Him. The whole time, Jesus remained silent before His accusers until charged under oath to respond to one final accusation. Though Jesus acquiesced, His response was brief and dismissive (Matt. 26:64).

King Herod also had an audience with Jesus that day. He had been hoping to see Jesus perform some miraculous sign, so he was pleased when Jesus was brought before him, because he was looking for an entertaining spectacle. But Jesus gave Herod no answer to his many questions, and refused to put on a show, much to the king's exasperation.

That leaves Pilate, the man who was easy to hate. He was a Gentile by birth and ceremonially unclean; even the Jewish leaders refused to enter his palace. He had slaughtered Jews on at least five occasions, until the emperor Tiberius finally called him to Rome to answer for his brutality.

As the governor reinforcing the Roman Empire's occupation of

Judea, Pilate deserved Jesus' hatred. As the man who failed to stand up to Jewish leaders, Pilate deserved Jesus' scorn. As the man who would condemn Jesus to death, Pilate deserved Jesus' condemnation.

Yet of the three men Jesus stood before that day, only Pilate received the privilege of an audience with the King of kings. Jesus' lengthy dialogue with Pilate stands in stark contrast with His sparse responses toward the others that day. Perhaps there was something special going on in their exchange—something that deserves slowing down and pondering.

Pilate's first question demonstrates his down-to-business attitude: "Are you the king of the Jews?" If Jesus responded yes, He would be admitting treason against Rome and His confession would be grounds for execution. But Jesus responds with a question, getting to the heart of the conversation: "Is that your own idea, or did others talk to you about me?" Jesus pushes past the allegation, intuiting what Pilate himself had heard and believed about Him.

Pilate tries again: "What is it you have done?" The Jewish leaders were obviously furious with Jesus, but Jesus was still drawing Pilate into a deeper conversation. He didn't directly answer Pilate's question; He wasn't defensive, even though He had every right to be. He didn't try to prove His innocence. He could have said, "I've walked the countryside for the past three years, calling people to love God and love one another, healing the sick, casting out demons, and bringing peace to the broken." He could have accused the Jewish leaders of pettiness and jealousy. He could have revealed hidden sins within the Jewish leaders to Pilate that would have led to their condemnation instead of His.

Yet Jesus remains in control of the conversation, pushing past superficialities to the heart of the matter, as He had with the Samaritan woman. Jesus keeps urging Pilate to face the truth about his own heart: "Everyone on the side of truth listens to me." After all, Jesus is the truth, the One who defines reality itself, and He stands accused by jealous leaders who can hardly scrape together enough lies to accuse Him.

Pilate's reaction is telling: "What is truth?" he retorts. Somehow, this prisoner bound before the governor manages to exude calm and control, while the one who's supposed to rule is scrambling to find a way out of the predicament. Pilate tries to reason with the Jewish leaders ("I find no basis for a charge"); he tries to barter with them ("Do you want me to release [him]?"); he tries to appease them ("Pilate took Jesus and had him flogged"); he tries to convince them ("I am bringing him out to you to let you know that I find no basis for a charge against him").

Yes, Jesus was committed to go to His death, but Pilate had a choice whether he would be a part of it. So Jesus draws Pilate into conversation through His quiet and calm demeanor, patiently reorienting Pilate's quest for truth to the greater reality of God's sovereign power and presence. He shatters Pilate's illusion of power, revealing that any authority he thinks he has came straight from the man he is facing. And He offers Pilate yet another clear statement of His innocence in Pilate's wife's troubling dream: "Don't have anything to do with that innocent man" (Matt. 27:19).

Jesus' invitation is extended. Pilate's choice is clear. But Jesus would not make his choice for him; just as in the garden of Eden, love demands free agency to choose for oneself whether to respond to love or act out of fear.

CHALLENGE

We know Pilate's choice, and we're each given a choice today. Jesus lovingly shatters our illusions of power and control, and reveals the fear we each cover up inside. Will we choose self-preservation or will we throw ourselves on the mercy of Jesus? Today, if you've never yielded to Jesus as your Lord and King, surrender to Him and receive His gift of life with Him forever.

PRAYER

"Search me, God, and know my heart; test me and know my anxious thoughts. See if there is any offensive way in me, and lead me in the way everlasting" (Ps. 139:23–24). Amen.

FOR FURTHER STUDY

Mark 15:5; John 18:28–19:16; 1 John 4:18

JESUS HONORS HIS MOTHER

When Jesus saw his mother there, and the disciple whom
he loved standing nearby, he said to her, "Woman, here is your son,"
and to the disciple, "Here is your mother." From that time on,
this disciple took her into his home.

JOHN 19:26–27

READ THE STORY: JOHN 19:23-27

Few things compare to the pain of watching a loved one suffer, unable to lift a finger to alleviate their agony. If you could take their place, you would. And yet, you can't.

We can only imagine Mary's pain as she stood at the foot of the cross, close enough to hear her firstborn Son's every rasping breath, to see the blood coming from His broken body, to witness His humiliation as He hung naked. The anguish must have pierced her heart, and the words of the prophet Simeon may have come to mind: "This child is destined to cause the falling and rising of many in Israel, and to be a sign that will be spoken against, so that the thoughts of many hearts will be revealed. And a sword will pierce your own soul too" (Luke 2:34–35).

How did Mary first react when she heard the old man speak those words in the temple courts all those years ago? Sleep-deprived and still reeling from the birth, Mary must have been shocked by the unexpected prophecy. But having cherished all these moments in her heart, she likely remembered those words as she grieved not far from her beloved Son.

Yet despite her soul-crushing desire to alleviate her Son's pain, the opposite actually takes place: Jesus takes her suffering on Himself and extends His loving care toward her. He sees her, and He speaks to her tenderly: "Woman, here is your son," He says, indicating the disciple He loved who was standing nearby. "Here is your mother," He says to John.

After hours of brutal torture and humiliating ridicule, Jesus locks His gaze on the two people He loved most, and ensures His mother would be well cared for. For yes, Jesus was a rabbi and the Messiah and the true King of Israel. But He was also a Son, and He honored His mother even in His death, perfectly fulfilling every letter of the law. This particular instruction is especially poignant in light of Jesus' rebuke of the Pharisees for neglecting to care for their parents in their self-righteous religious zeal (see Mark 7:9–13). Jesus would have none of that. Honoring our heavenly Father flows into honoring one's earthly parents as well.

From this exchange, we surmise that Mary was a widow, and as the oldest son in a Jewish family, it was Jesus' responsibility to care for His mother. Jesus provided Mary with someone who would care not only for her physical needs, but for her spiritual and emotional needs, especially in the days following His death. She would grieve deeply, and she needed someone who loved Jesus deeply to support her in the days to come.

Hanging on the cross, Jesus fulfilled His last duty toward His mother, thus demonstrating steadfast love toward her, honoring her even moments before His death.

CHALLENGE

In a society that prizes youth, energy, and productivity, older generations can feel sidelined. But Jesus' way of love reveals that love honors parents, even in death. Whether your parents are still living or they've passed on, how can you honor them today? Also, look around you: is there a parent figure in your community who lacks adult children to care for them? How might you love them like John was tasked with loving and caring for Mary?

PRAYER

Jesus, You never cease to surprise me with Your outpouring of love. I want to love and honor my parents and those older generations You've placed in my life. Show me how to love older men as fathers and older women as mothers, giving proper respect and honor to those who have lived longer than me. Help me model a humble and selfless love toward them, so that younger generations may watch and learn Your love through me. Amen.

FOR FURTHER STUDY

Exodus 20:12; Deuteronomy 5:16; Proverbs 23:22;
Matthew 15:1–9; 1 Timothy 5:1–8; James 1:27

JESUS OFFERS HOPE

Then he said, "Jesus, remember me when you
come into your kingdom." Jesus answered him,
"Truly I tell you, today you will be with me in paradise."

LUKE 23:42–43

READ THE STORY: LUKE 23:32–43

One of the most surprising conversions in the New Testament is that of the criminal hanging beside Jesus on the cross.

To fulfill Old Testament prophecy, Jesus was hung between two criminals; though we don't know for sure what their crimes were, we do know that crucifixion was reserved for the most heinous offenders.

These two men on Jesus' right and left were no tender folk. In fact, Scripture records that they were both heaping insults on Jesus, joining the crowds in charging Him to get off the cross and save Himself—perhaps them too.

But at some point, one of the criminals stops jeering and realizes that the man hanging next to him is, in fact, the Son of God.

He and the other man were dying rightfully for their crimes; but this man, he realizes, is innocent.

When did he recognize he was wrong in his mockery? And what emotions would have flooded his soul? Shame? Humiliation? Grief? . . . Fear?

He turns to the other criminal and rebukes him. "Don't you fear God?" he asks. "This man has done nothing wrong."

And with the most simple prayer of faith ever spoken, he turns to Jesus and asks Him to remember him when Jesus comes into His kingdom. How and when that would happen, he was unsure. But he realized who the victor was, and he wanted to be on His side in the end.

It is surprising to see such an abrupt turn from scoffing to supplication.

Would Jesus acquiesce?

Each breath would have been labored, as they pulled themselves up to fill their ragged lungs. We can imagine the criminal waited to hear Jesus' reply—each word deliberate—each breath piercing.

"Truly . . . I tell you . . ."

What? What is Jesus going to say? Will He call down fire from heaven to burn up this criminal? Or will He show mercy even in His dying moments?

"Today you will be with me in paradise."

Jesus accepted the criminal's last-minute faith, showing that as long as you have breath, it's never too late to turn to Him.

But what's more, the criminal had asked only to be "remembered" when Jesus begins His reign. But Jesus goes above and beyond the criminal's request, promising that he will join Jesus in paradise, not at some distant point in the future but "today."

Because to Jesus, no one is beyond hope of salvation. And because *of* Jesus, we have hope to the very end of our days.

CHALLENGE

Oftentimes we do things we're not proud of, and these sins cause us to hide in secret. But Jesus welcomes us to shed the shame and guilt and enter into His presence with Him. Today, confess those sins that stand between you and fellowship with God, and celebrate His great love that goes above and beyond anything we can ask for or imagine.

PRAYER

Lord Jesus, You are so, so good. You were merciful toward that criminal on the cross, and You are merciful with me today. Thank You for such undeserved love. I confess my sins to You and receive Your forgiveness. May I walk in the joy of Your presence today. Amen.

FOR FURTHER STUDY

Isaiah 53:12; Mark 15:32; Ephesians 3:20

JESUS' LOVE FORGIVES

Jesus said, "Father, forgive them,
for they do not know what they are doing."

LUKE 23:34

Bear with each other and forgive one another if any of you
has a grievance against someone. Forgive as the Lord forgave you.
And over all these virtues put on love,
which binds them all together in perfect unity.

COLOSSIANS 3:13–14

READ THE STORY: LUKE 23:32–34

As He hung dying on the cross, Jesus forgave His executioners. We would expect nothing less of Him—He is, after all, the Son of God.

But when we look at the prevailing cultural norms of His day, we begin to understand just how unexpected His prayer of forgiveness would have been for first-century listeners—both those standing at the foot of His cross and those hearing the account of His death.

Through Israel's history, family members were entreated to avenge an innocent person's death. God Himself instructed the Israelites to show no pity toward murderers but to expunge them through capital punishment. A life for a life. That seemed just.

In those cases where revenge was beyond human means, faithful worshipers pleaded with God to exact judgment and vindication when they couldn't. In fact, there are over thirty imprecatory psalms—calling for divine judgment and vindication. It was normal to want revenge. It was biblical to ask God to enact justice. And if an innocent Jewish man were hanging from a Roman cross, you could be sure that he would be calling down God's wrath on his executioners.

But not Jesus.

After being crucified between two criminals, Jesus' first recorded words in Luke are this prayer of forgiveness. Typically, a person being executed was expected to confess his sins, usually posted on a charge sheet at the head of the cross. Jesus' charge sheet read, "Jesus of Nazareth, the King of the Jews" (John 19:19), the inscription bearing more truth than Pilate could even realize.

But it wasn't His own sins that Jesus confessed on the cross. After all, He had none. Instead, He confessed His executioners' sins and pleaded for their forgiveness.

This was the way of love He had taught His disciples to walk, when He told them to bless those who curse them and pray for those who mistreat them. Forgiveness that reflects the Father's heart of love knows no limits.

Yet Jesus demonstrates His love for the very men who nailed Him to the cross, not just freely granting His own forgiveness but also praying to His heavenly Father for their absolution.

These words spoken from the cross would have been shocking indeed. If anyone deserved to hold a grudge, it was Jesus. If anyone was justified in calling down divine judgment on His executioners, it was Jesus. Consider the prophet Zechariah's stoning in the Old Testament, killed for delivering God's warning to King Joash. As he lay dying, he prayed, "May the LORD see this and call you to account" (2 Chron. 24:22). On Zechariah's mind was not forgiveness, but justice and revenge, perhaps clinging to God's promise: "It is mine to avenge. I will repay" (Deut. 32:35).

In contrast, Jesus shows that love forgives, not because it hasn't been wronged, but because it trusts in the One who can make all things right. Jesus didn't want His executioners condemned as Zechariah had been—He wanted them redeemed.

And from the cross, hanging by the nails these men had pounded into His hands and feet, Jesus looks upon them with compassion and prays for their forgiveness.

CHALLENGE

Such forgiveness surpasses human ability to love. It can only be divine. Yet soon after Jesus' ascension to heaven, we hear the first Christian martyr, Stephen, praying those same words of forgiveness for his own executioners (see Acts 7:60). Who in your life do you need to forgive? Pray for them today, using Jesus' and Stephen's prayers as models, and ask God to uncover His love in your heart toward them.

PRAYER

Lord Jesus, You have shown such mercy and love toward those men who didn't deserve Your forgiveness. And You've shown that same love toward me. Thank You for forgiving me when I was still Your enemy. Release in me Your healing power of forgiveness, and help me love and forgive as You have done. Amen.

FOR FURTHER STUDY

Genesis 9:5; Deuteronomy 19:13, 21; 27:24–25; 32:35;
2 Chronicles 24:20–22; Psalms 69, 94; Luke 6:37; 11:4; 17:4;
Acts 7:54–60

JESUS SACRIFICED EVERYTHING

"Greater love has no one than this:
to lay down one's life for one's friends."

JOHN 15:13

Very rarely will anyone die for a righteous person, though for a good
person someone might possibly die. But God demonstrates his own
love for us in this: While we were still sinners, Christ died for us.

ROMANS 5:7–8

READ THE STORY: JOHN 19:16–30

My five-year-old knows that Jesus died on a cross, much like many of us did at her age, but she doesn't yet understand the tragedy of it all. And I fear sometimes that for us as adults, biblical knowledge about Jesus becomes so familiar that it fails to move us to worship.

Imagine, instead, a completely different scenario than the one you know so well: What if Jesus had been decapitated by the sword?

What if He had been burned at the stake?

What if He had been thrown to wild animals?

How would that change our perception of His death? Would it move you with compassion? Dread? Injustice? Pity?

Each of these methods of execution is gruesome, and we shudder when we read accounts of early church martyrs killed in those ways. But crucifixion was considered a more painful and disgraceful form of capital punishment than any of the above. If slaves and criminals could choose, they would choose *anything but* death on the cross.[1]

Under the Roman Empire, crucifixion was reserved for executing foreigners, lower-class Romans, violent offenders, and traitors. The condemned were often scourged until the soldier could lash out no more. They were forced to march through the city naked, stripped of dignity and pride. Other forms of torture and ridicule were common, as we read about in all the gospel accounts—the soldiers blindfolded Jesus and beat Him, demanding that He prophesy who punched Him; shoving a twisted garland of a thorny shrub onto His head; throwing an elegant robe over His tattered shoulders; striking Him with the staff they had given Him as a scepter; kneeling before Him with mock salutations, "Hail, king of the Jews!" before rising to spit in His face.

The whole of it is too gruesome to imagine.

Pilate's soldiers, Herod's guards, and even the Jewish leaders tortured and humiliated Jesus, and all this was before the Roman soldiers mounted Him on a cross, driving spikes through His hands and feet, thrusting Him up to hang on a roughly hewn stake in the ground, leaving Him to pull Himself up to gasp for each breath of air. Crucified victims couldn't chase away birds or flies from their wounds, couldn't restrain their bodily fluids, and couldn't protect themselves from the scorching heat of the day and the shivering cold of the night. What's more, crosses were often hung low enough that dogs could try to eat the victim's feet.

It's too much.

The brutality and utter depravity of such an execution is too much for our modern sensibilities, so we turn our faces. Who could look upon such torture and not feel sick to their stomach?

But the worst moment was yet to come: Jesus' own Father turns His face away from His Son. Every sin of every person from all time past, present, and future—even the crimes of those executing Him—were heaped upon His innocent soul. The perfect spotless Lamb of God was being slaughtered for the sins of the world in the most abhorrent and shameful way.

But unlike the two criminals hanging with Him, Jesus was not a powerless prisoner. With a single flex of His muscles He could have healed His own wounds and come down from that cross; a single whisper would have called down legions of warrior angels; a single command and the enemy would be obliterated. What, then, kept Jesus on the cross?

You know the answer, don't you?

But feel the weight of it.

Love.

Every blow He didn't reciprocate was love. Every moment He stood naked and mocked was love. Every step toward Golgotha was love. Every gasping breath was love. Every nanosecond from the kiss in the garden to the cessation of His heartbeat . . . love.

CHALLENGE AND PRAYER

In lieu of a challenge and written prayer today, spend time being silent before the cross. Allow the spectacle of the cross to imprint on your soul the weight of Jesus' love. Don't rush this. Witness your own sins heaped on Jesus and grieve this heinous moment in history. Then reread today's devotional, pausing wherever you feel the need to respond with sorrow, repentance, adoration, and tears.

FOR FURTHER STUDY

Isaiah 52:13–53:12; Matthew 26:67–68; 27:22–50; Mark 14:65; 15:12–37; Luke 22:63–65, 23:11–46; John 18:22–23; 19:1–37; 2 Corinthians 5:21; Revelation 5:12

*E*ver wonder how to keep Easter centered on Jesus? The activities below range from hands-on crafts that help you better understand Scripture to new spins on ancient disciplines like fasting, prayer, and almsgiving. They can be used by adults or adapted for children. Pick one or more activities to prepare your heart to celebrate Jesus this Easter.

* **Prepare a Passover Seder** to commemorate the special meal that Jesus and His disciples ate on that last night. You can make it a simple family meal or an extravagant fellowship event. Find detailed instructions at uncoveringthelove.com.

* **Wash each other's feet** using a large bowl, a kitchen towel, and a pitcher of water. Read John 13:1–16 and discuss how Jesus wants us to serve one another in love.

* **Discuss the Last Supper** while breaking bread and drinking grape juice together. Take turns reading Luke 22:7–20. You can also mold playdough into a loaf of bread and a cup to remember the elements of communion. Place them out to dry at your Lenten station.

* **Consider a total or partial fast on Good Friday,** from Thursday dinner until Friday dinner, to com-

memorate the suffering of our Lord Jesus. Use the time you'd typically spend preparing food and eating to read the crucifixion account in the gospel of your choice. Invite family members to participate as they are able and willing.

- **Turn off the lights** from 3 p.m. on Good Friday to Resurrection Sunday morning, to symbolize the spiritual darkness that covered the earth during Jesus' death. On resurrection morning, flip on the lights in all the house to symbolize the bright glory of Jesus' resurrection.

BONUS CONTENT

Go to uncoveringthelove.com to find step-by-step tutorials, download a free printable activity sheet, and discover other helpful resources to observe Lent together as a family.

RESURRECTION SUNDAY

f you're going through this devotional with your family, you can visit uncoveringthelove.com, print out the questions and Scripture readings on separate slips of paper, and distribute them among your family members in order to involve everyone. Most of these components are simple enough for even small children to read alone or with help.

OPEN WITH A SIMPLE PRAYER.

READ THE FOLLOWING VERSES ALOUD:

> "Since the children have flesh and blood, he too shared in their humanity so that by his death he might break the power of him who holds the power of death—that is, the devil—and free those who all their lives were held in slavery by their fear of death." — Hebrews 2:14–15

SOMEONE ASKS:

> Why did Jesus have to die?

SOMEONE RESPONDS:

> Jesus died to achieve eternal victory over death through His resurrection!

LIGHT ALL THE CANDLES ON YOUR LENTEN WREATH, IF USING ONE.

John 20:11–18

DISCUSSION QUESTIONS:

1. Throughout the Bible we read of people who were resurrected by God's prophets. But Jesus is the only One who raised Himself from the dead without the intervention of any other person. What does this tell us about Jesus?

2. Jesus appears to Mary at the tomb and reveals Himself by saying her name. How have you personally experienced Jesus' love toward you?

3. How does Jesus' resurrection victory compel you to love others in your life?

SING THE FOLLOWING SONG TOGETHER:

"Christ the Lord Is Risen Today" by Charles Wesley (1739)

JESUS HAS RISEN!

"Do not be afraid, for I know that you are looking for Jesus, who was crucified. He is not here; he has risen, just as he said."

MATTHEW 28:5–6

f I live to be a hundred, I'll never get over the beauty of that history-changing declaration.

Jesus Christ has risen!

He has risen, indeed.

And this is the best news of all because despite our mortal enemy's best attempt, Jesus' cross was not a place of defeat but of victory—the triumph of love over sin and death!

I hope that news never gets old for you.

I hope these last few weeks reflecting on the life and love of Jesus have changed something in you when you say those words.

I hope you've found yourself in these familiar Bible stories, the recipient of Jesus' extravagant, never-stopping, never-giving-up love.

I hope you've grown to know Jesus as a person and as God and to love Him more than ever before.

I hope you've experienced His love filling you up and spilling over into the most surprising relationships.

I hope you've found space to grieve and mourn and lament . . . and also to hope and celebrate and rejoice, all because of Jesus.

This is the beauty of Lent: its cadence allows space for the whole spectrum of human emotion, its narrative arc leading us through desolation to the triumphant conclusion of Jesus' resurrection that is just the beginning.

But every year **I'm surprised by how quickly it's all over.**

Especially after weeks of waiting, watching, and preparing throughout Lent, Resurrection Sunday comes with all its joyous celebration, and before we know it, Monday's here and we're back to our regular routines.

But I realized something the year I wrote this devotional: **it doesn't have to be this way.**

In fact, believers throughout history have continued celebrating Jesus' resurrection during the fifty days leading up to Pentecost, and we can too. **Because as we continue to remind ourselves of the reality of Jesus' resurrection, we begin to live the lives of the resurrected.**

I've suggested a few activities on the next pages to help you celebrate the joy of Jesus' resurrection this week, but let me encourage you to keep coming back to this book in the weeks and months to come. Continue to remind yourself of the deep, deep love of Jesus, and continue to ask for His love to pour out into the lives of others.

Don't let the celebration end, friend. Jesus has risen!

And because He lives, we can face tomorrow, and the day after that, with hope.

With much joy,

Asheritah

RESURRECTION WEEK ACTIVITIES

Ever feel like Easter is over too quickly? Pick one or more activities to continue celebrating our risen Jesus in the weeks following Easter.

✱ **Read the gospel accounts of Jesus' death and resurrection over and over again**. Don't let this story get old. Read it in different translations. Read it out loud and listen to it read. Read a historical novel version. Act it out or draw it out.

✱ **Watch a visual retelling of the life of Jesus**, like the word-for-word dramatic presentations of the Gospels from Lumo, available in the YouVersion Bible app in twelve languages.

✱ **Write out the resurrection account** from one of the Gospels in your own handwriting, pausing to savor the story and letting it penetrate your heart.

✱ **Hold an Easter egg knocking competition around the table.** This Romanian tradition is one my family continues to observe each year, inviting guests to join in the fun. Each person chooses a dyed egg and turns to the person sitting next to them. The first says, "Christ has risen!" And the other responds, "He has risen indeed!" Then the first person knocks the top of their egg to the bottom of the other's egg. Whoever's egg remains uncracked proceeds to the next round. Continue knocking eggs with the Easter greeting until the last uncracked egg remains.

✳ **Bake resurrection rolls to visualize Jesus' resurrection.** Like any illustration, this will never capture the immensity of the miracle of Jesus coming back to life, but for little children trying to understand the resurrection, it does capture the wonder of the empty tomb. Dip marshmallows in butter and cinnamon sugar, wrap in crescent dough, and bake according to package directions. As you work together, read the crucifixion and burial account in Luke 23:26–56 or the *Jesus Storybook Bible*. Discuss how Jesus' body was prepared for burial and then placed in the tomb. As the rolls are baking, read the resurrection account in Luke 24:1–12. The marshmallows will puff up during baking, but once the rolls have cooled, the marshmallows will have disappeared completely.

✳ **Donate extra candy to charities** like Ronald McDonald House, Operation Shoebox, local homeless shelters, and foster homes.

✳ **Set a reminder on your calendar to hold on to your Christmas tree this winter.** After you've taken down the Christmas decorations, hack off the branches and carve a simple cross out of the wood to use as a Lenten wreath the following year. This activity helps children connect our celebration of Jesus coming into the world at Christmastime with His death on the cross at Easter. (You can find additional Christmas family activities at unwrappingthenames.com.)

✳ **Host an Easter Art Show.** Invite friends and family to bring their Lenten crafts, coloring pages, and Easter art to show and tell what you've learned throughout the Lenten season. Share how you've grown to understand Jesus' love for you, and how you experienced His love poured out as you served others.

BONUS CONTENT

Go to uncoveringthelove.com to find step-by-step tutorials, download a free printable activity sheet, and discover other helpful resources to observe Lent together as a family.

ACKNOWLEDGMENTS

Precious Jesus, Your love still amazes me. I'm ecstatic for the day You're coming back so I can thank You face-to-face. Soon.

Frumosu Meu, you've seen it all and you love me still. *Te iubesc.* Together for His glory, forever.

Carissa, Amelia, and Theo, being your mom has taught me so much about the love of Jesus. You're His precious gifts to me, and I love you with all my heart.

Wendy, your spoken prayers covered me and my family from a thousand miles away when I had no strength to pray. Words are not enough.

Judy, Amanda, and the Moody Publishers team, thank you for saying "yes" to another book (though this was the hardest yet). I'm forever grateful for your partnership in the gospel.

Dear reader, I pictured this little book in your hands as I wrote each page. May the love of Jesus become sweeter to you with each passing day, until we see Him face-to-face.

NOTES

WHY OBSERVE LENT?

1. As a millennial myself, I can attest to my own attraction to ancient church traditions that are often absent from contemporary evangelical church services, as well as the troubling feeling that such a desire somehow betrays the sacrifice of Reformation-era brothers and sisters who have gone before me. The conversation surrounding a proper appropriation of Lenten practices is deeper and richer than would fit in this brief introduction. So let me refer you to the excellent book *The Good of Giving Up: Discovering the Freedom of Lent* (Chicago: Moody, 2017) by Aaron Damiani for an accessible exploration of the history of Lent and an evangelical case for its practice in our church communities today. See "A (Mercifully Short) History of Lent," 35–36.

2. A fantastic resource on this topic is John Piper's book *Fifty Reasons Why Jesus Came to Die* (Wheaton, IL: Crossway, 2006).

3. One of the most common hang-ups for beginners of Lent is not knowing when it starts and how long it lasts. To clarify, the season of Lent spans the forty-six days preceding Easter Sunday; since Sundays are considered mini-celebrations of Jesus' resurrection, they are excluded from the traditional requirements of fasting, which is why Lent is commonly referred to as forty days long. To determine the start of Lent each year, use a calendar or type "when does Lent begin in [current year]" in your preferred search engine.

4. At the time I began drafting this book, I sensed the Lord lay someone on my heart so that I may live out this uncovering of Jesus' love in my own life before I wrote about it. I knew I wanted to love them better, but I didn't know where to start. My friend Wendy suggested I plan acts of love based on Gary Chapman's work in the weeks leading up to Easter. She emphasized that just because a loving act is preplanned does not make it any less sincere, and that in time my feelings may

follow my actions. She was right. I was pleasantly surprised to notice a thawing of both our hearts as Jesus' love compelled me to practical love. We may become closer in the years to come; conversely, it's possible that we will never be best buddies. In any case, I've personally experienced the power of God's love to change us as we respond to His love, and I believe you will experience restoration and redemption in your relationships as well. For more information, see: Gary Chapman, *The 5 Love Languages* (Chicago: Northfield, 2015).

WEEK 1

1. My understanding of Jesus' temptation expanded as I listened to this excellent sermon from the co-creator of The Bible Project: Tim Mackie, n.d., "Testing Jesus in the Wilderness, Gospel of Matthew Part 3," podcast audio, *Exploring My Strange Bible*, May 14, 2018, https://exploring-my-strange-bible.simplecast.com/episodes/921dab20-921dab20.

2. "In first-century Palestine, disciples typically took the initiative in attaching themselves to a particular rabbi, not vice versa. As a well-known dictum declared, 'Provide yourself with a teacher.' Jesus broke with this custom and called his own disciples" (R. M. Bowman Jr., "Is Jesus the Only Way?," *CSB Study Bible*, E. A. Blum and T. Wax, eds. [Nashville: Holman Bible Publishers, 2017], 1698).

3. To better understand how the rabbis of Jesus' day would have viewed His disciples, see the temple rulers' opinion of Peter and John in Acts 4:13.

4. According to one scholar, "Running out of wine represented a social disaster much greater in the first century than it would today. Disgrace, humiliation, insult—all these and more would be brought upon the family with such carelessness as to allow this to happen. Wedding celebrations in that day sometimes lasted nearly a week, so the wine supply was a major consideration." For more, see: Kenneth O. Gangel, *John*, Holman New Testament Commentary, vol. 4 (Nashville: Broadman & Holman, 2000).

WEEK 2

1. I don't usually wade into textual criticism, but this one's worth pondering, because it reveals something of Jesus' character in Mark 1:41. While most English translations (including the KJV, ESV, HCSB, and NLT) refer to Jesus' compassion or pity (original Greek word *splagchnizomai*; Strong's G4697), the NIV pulls from a few

other ancient manuscripts that render the verse as "Jesus was indignant." The variation comes from weighing external and internal evidence in deciding which manuscripts to translate. Elsewhere in the gospel narratives, we see examples of both Jesus' compassion and His indignation, and both responses are plausible. Most commentators on the gospel of Mark opine that the original Greek text refers to Jesus' anger, explaining that it's His divine response to seeing His perfect creation twisted and disfigured by the effects of sin. This response makes sense within the context of Jesus' righteous anger at sin's effect on His world (see Week Five, Day Three for a discussion on Jesus' anger), yet it doesn't invalidate His response of compassion toward this man who had been thus disfigured. Both responses are appropriate; both express His love. To read more about the Bible translators' decision-making process on Mark 1:41, read: Louis, "Was Jesus Angry or Compassionate According to Mark 1:41? The NIV vs. NLT," *The Baker Deep End Blog*, Baker Book House, bbhchurchconnection.wordpress.com/2012/09/10/was-jesus-angry-or-compassionate-according-to-mark-141-the-niv-vs-nlt.

2. "splagchnizomai," Blue Letter Bible, Strong's G4697, www.blueletterbible.org/lang/lexicon/lexicon.cfm?Strongs=G4697&t=KJV.

WEEK 3

1. The Old Testament prophets frequently referred to Israel's royal and priestly administrators as the nation's shepherds, accusing them of abusing their power and failing to provide and protect the people. In Mark 6:14–29, the passage immediately preceding today's text, King Herod throws a drunken, lustful, and murderous banquet; the contrast between that meal and Jesus' benevolent banquet in Mark 6:30–44 would not have been lost on original readers.

2. A bit of historical background may prove helpful here: "Apparitions were usually frightening (though Josephus employs the term here translated "ghost" for angels). Jewish tradition warned of dangerous night spirits. On a popular level, many Gentiles and probably a number of Jews believed in ghosts, although such a belief technically contradicts mainstream Jewish views of the afterlife (heaven or hell and future resurrection). Gentiles often believed that the ghosts of those drowned at sea hovered over the sites of their deaths" (*NIV Cultural Backgrounds Study Bible*, footnote on Matthew 14:26, eds. David W. Baker, et al. [Grand Rapids: Zondervan, 2016]).

3. *The Moody Bible Commentary* is helpful here: "When Jesus said **it is I**, the Gk. words are *ego eimi*, a phrase used in Isaiah 40–50 (LXX) by God when He alone claims to have the power to rescue His people. . . . Is 41:10 says, 'Do not fear ["fear" here is *phobou*; in Mt 14:27, *phobeisthe*—same word, different person and mood], for I am with you; Do not anxiously look about you, for I am [ego eimi] your God. . . . Surely I will uphold you with My righteous right hand'" (Michael G. Vanlaningham, "Matthew," in *The Moody Bible Commentary*, Michael Rydelnik and Michael Vanlaningham, eds. [Chicago: Moody, 2014], 1479).

4. I've found myself wondering what exactly Peter was doubting in that moment. We can't know for sure, but I wonder if Peter doubted whether Jesus would save him from the crashing waves. Had he doubted one time too many? Yes, Jesus was God. Yes, Jesus had power over nature. Yes, Jesus could save him. But would He? We can easily put ourselves in Peter's shaky sandals: Am I worthy of Jesus' love? Am I worthy of being saved, after I got myself into this mess? Will Jesus give me a second chance? Or a third? Or a fourth? Whether these thoughts crossed Peter's mind we'll never know. But the answer to all those questions is a resounding "Yes!" Jesus' ongoing love and compassion for Peter is proof of that (see Luke 22:32; John 21:15–19).

WEEK 4

1. "It was long since the law of death had been demanded; and even had this not been the case, the Roman law would have interfered" (J. S. Exell, *The Biblical Illustrator: St. John*, Vol. 2 [London: James Nisbet & Co., n.d.], 5–6). Both the *The Biblical Illustrator: St. John* and *New Bible Commentary: 21st Century Edition* support that the Jewish leaders did not have the legal right to execute anyone without the governor's permission (see John 18:31), but it seems Roman rulers may have occasionally allowed stoning as long as it didn't result in a public disturbance (as in Stephen's case) (John D. Guthrie, *New Bible Commentary: 21st Century Edition*, 4th ed., D. A. Carson, R. T. France, J. A. Motyer, and G. J. Wenham, eds. [Leicester, England; Downers Grove, IL: InterVarsity Press, 1994], 1061).

WEEK 5

1. This theological phrase, originally *incurvatus in se* in Latin, is thought to have originated with the early church theologian Augustine of Hippo, though it appears in Paul's writings in Romans 7:15–19 and was also expounded upon by Martin

Luther in his *Lectures on Romans* as well as Karl Barth and Søren Kierkegaard. This phrase provides a basic paradigm that helps us understand sin and its effects not just personally but also relationally, describing a life lived inward for oneself rather than outward for God and others. Though such a discussion is outside the scope of this book, the Lenten season offers us a beautiful opportunity to meditate on the effects of such sin in our lives. I'm convinced we need to develop a better vocabulary to discuss sin so that we may continue to mortify it, both personally and relationally. A hefty but helpful starter may be Matt Jenson's book *The Gravity of Sin: Augustine, Luther, and Barth on* 'Homo Incurvatus in Se' (London: T & T Clark, 2006).

2. As a "chief" tax collector, Zacchaeus would have set collection policies and hired other tax collectors to work for him. He would have been held accountable by his people for the misdeeds of all those under his supervision. For more information, see Craig S. Keener's "The Gospel of Luke" in the *NIV Cultural Backgrounds Study Bible*, eds. David W. Baker et al. (Grand Rapids: Zondervan, 2016), 1787.

3. In this Middle Eastern culture, offering hospitality to a renowned teacher was a great honor, but respected teachers didn't request hospitality. So Jesus tramples over all sorts of unwritten rules as He extends friendship to this scorned man.

4. John MacArthur, *1 Corinthians*, The MacArthur New Testament Commentary series (Chicago: Moody, 1984), 353.

WEEK 6

1. The perfume in question cost a year's wages, which would amount to a lifetime's savings. In today's economy at the current minimum wage, that would bring the cost to approximately $25,000. This exact figure comes from John Piper's sermon "Leave Her Alone, Judas—This Is for My Burial," on November 5, 2011 at Bethlehem Baptist Church, https://www.desiringgod.org/messages/leave-her-alone-judas-this-is-for-my-burial. Another scholarly resource that supports this figure is Donald Guthrie's "John" in the *New Bible Commentary: 21st Century Edition*, ed. D. A. Carson, R. T. France, J. A. Motyer, and G. J. Wenham, 4th ed., 1051. Leicester, England (Downers Grove, IL: InterVarsity Press, 1994).

2. See Exodus 21:32 for the redemption cost of a slave. Zechariah 11:12 uses the same phrase for the "wages" paid to the rejected shepherd (the Messiah), and Matthew refers to this prophecy in 27:9–10. The exact value of thirty pieces of silver is disputable, with some scholars stating that it could be up to four months' wages

and others as little as a single month. Regardless of the exact amount, Judas scoffs at Mary's extravagant offering for Jesus while betraying Him for a fraction of that cost. For more details, see Louis A. Barbieri, Jr.'s "Matthew," in *The Bible Knowledge Commentary: An Exposition of the Scriptures*, ed. J. F. Walvoord and R. B. Zuck, 2:82 (Wheaton, IL: Victor Books, 1985).

3. Craig S. Keener, "The Gospel of John," *NIV Cultural Backgrounds Study Bible*, eds. David W. Baker et al. (Grand Rapids: Zondervan, 2016), 1841.

WEEK 7

1. Craig S. Keener, *NIV Cultural Backgrounds Study Bible*, eds. David W. Baker et al. (Grand Rapids: Zondervan, 2016), 1852.

More from Asheritah Ciuciu

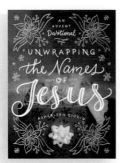

978-0-8024-1672-8

An Advent devotional to help the whole family be worshipful throughout the season.

978-0-8024-1935-4

31 devotional prompts and 31 healthy and tasty breakfast recipes to start your morning off right.

978-0-8024-1537-0

Unpacks a theology of food to help readers engage it biblically and holistically.

978-0-8024-1686-5

A 6-week study of Colossians on the life-altering importance of Jesus' sufficiency and sovereignty.

Also available as eBooks

MOODY Publishers®

From the Word to Life®

ONE THING ALONE
MINISTRIES

We help women enjoy
time with Jesus every day

Discover simple ways to find joy in Jesus through
creative and consistent time in His Word.

Start Today
onethingalone.com